I0756150

Bangkok:
Colors of the Beaten Path

Bangkok:
Colors of the Beaten Path

Rob Benton

Esotericom®

All photographs by Rob Benton

ISBN 978-0-9980682-2-0

BANGKOK . . .

EVERYWHERE YOU POINT YOUR CAMERA,

THERE'S A PICTURE.

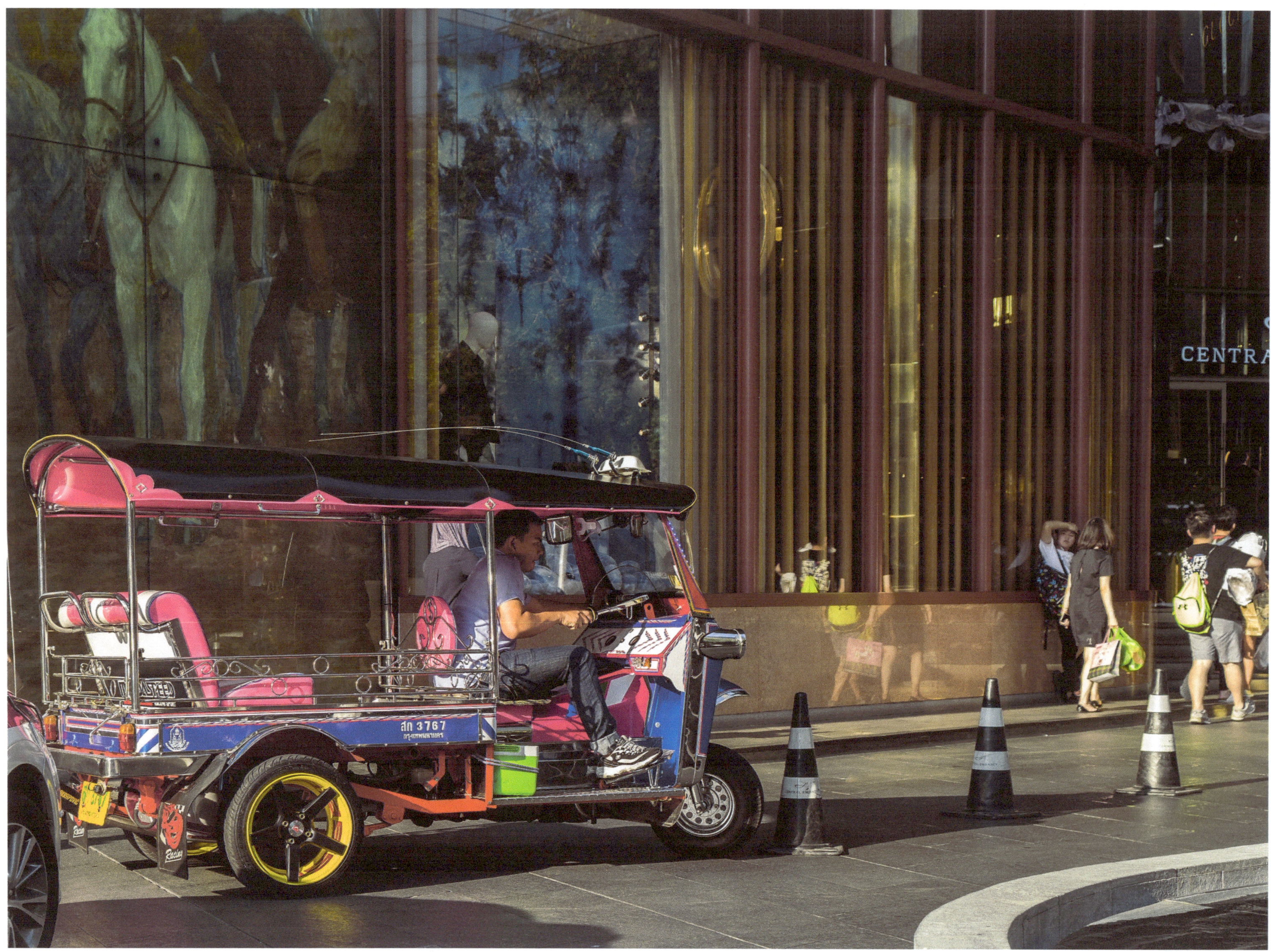
CENTRA
สก 3767

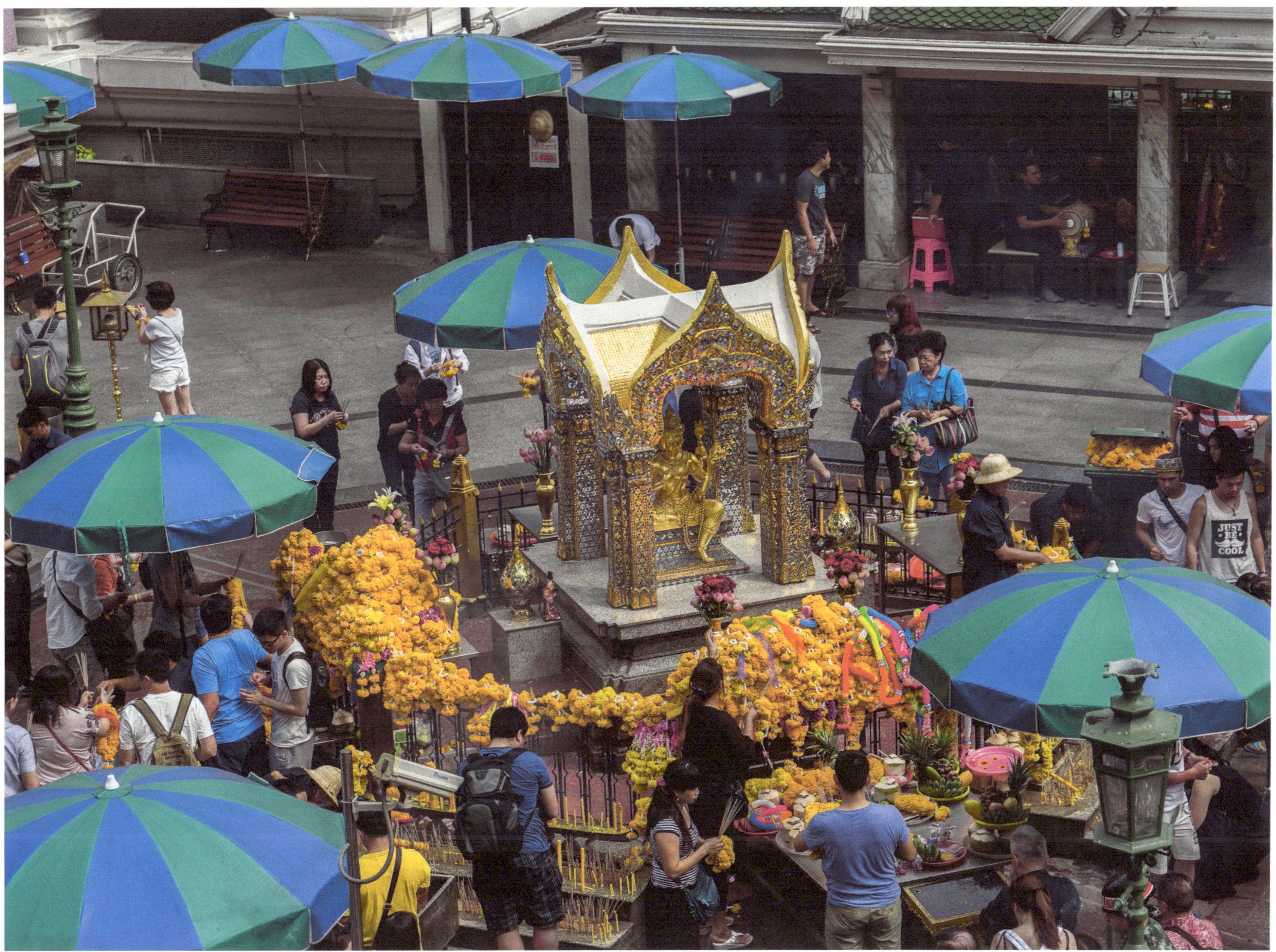
JUST
BE
COOL

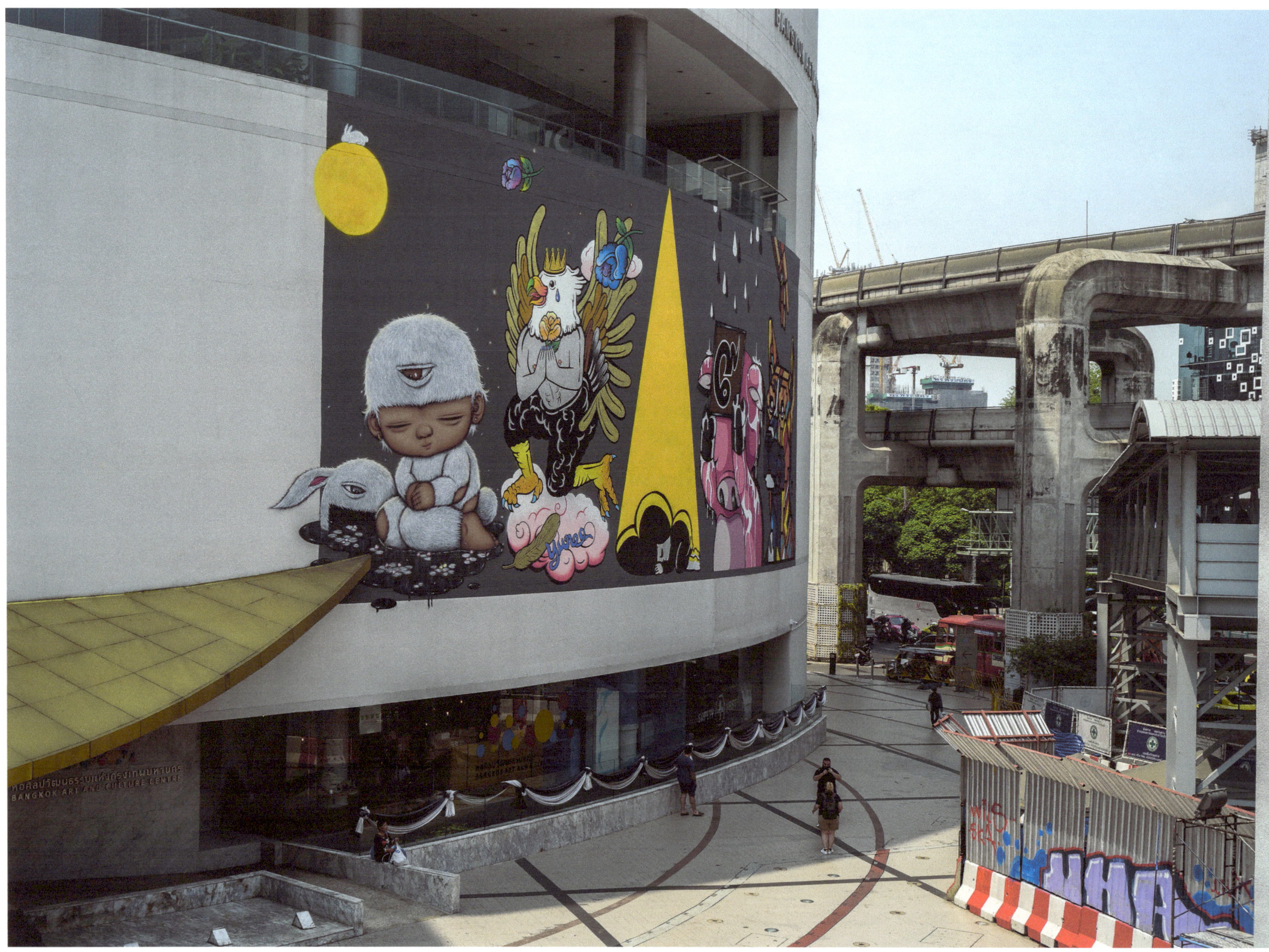
หอศิลปวัฒนธรรมแห่งกรุงเทพมหานคร
BANGKOK ART AND CULTURE CENTRE

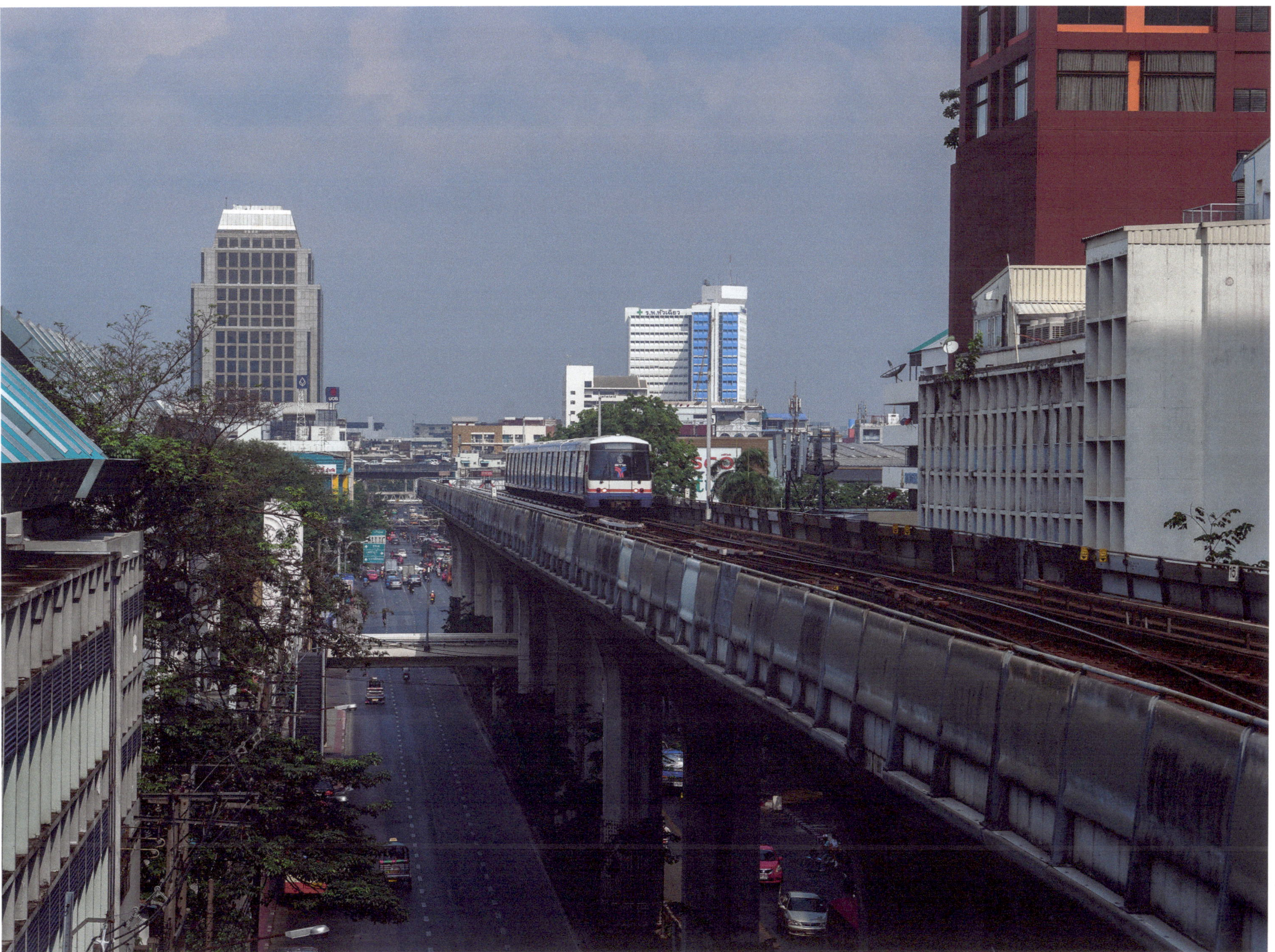

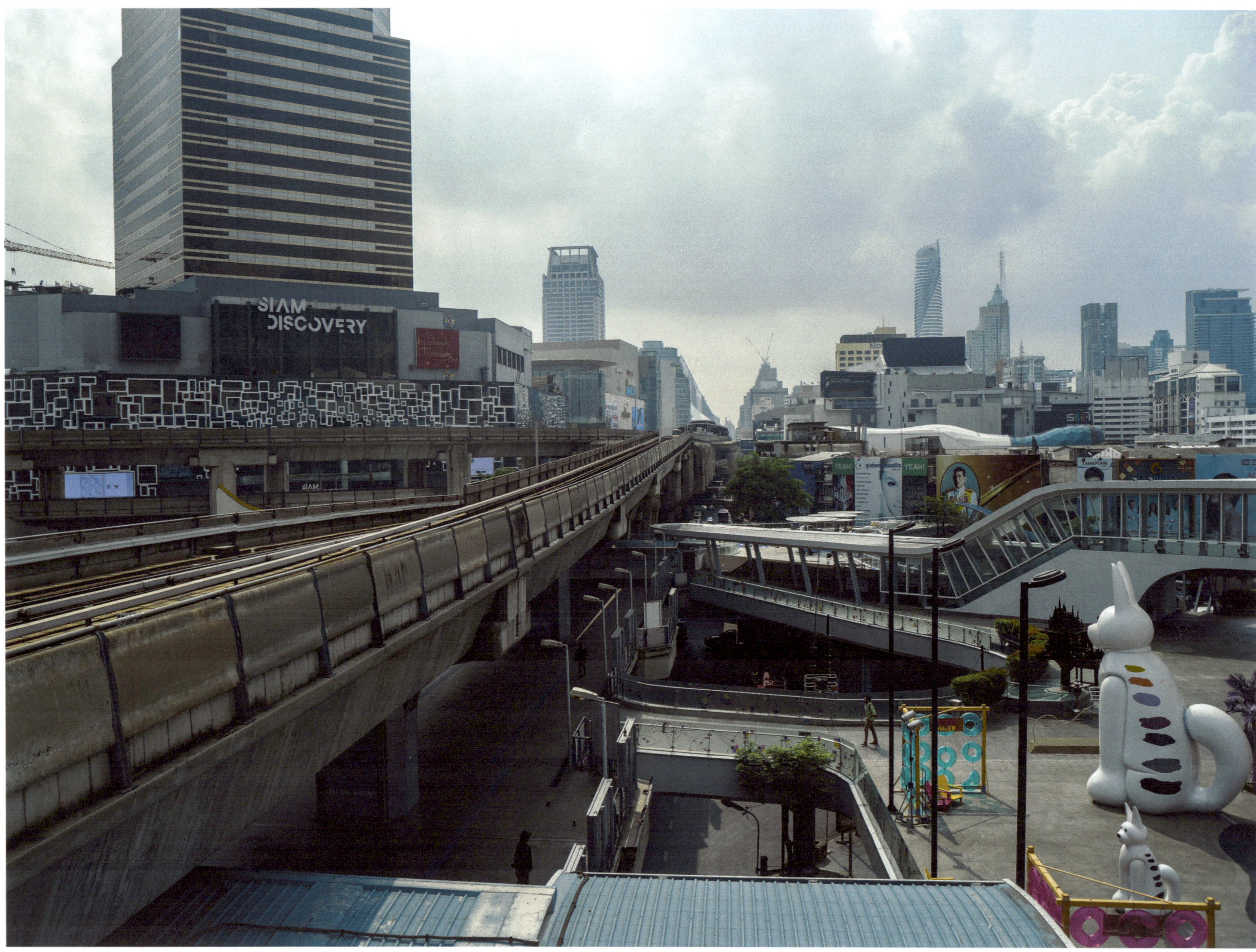
SIAM
DISCOVERY

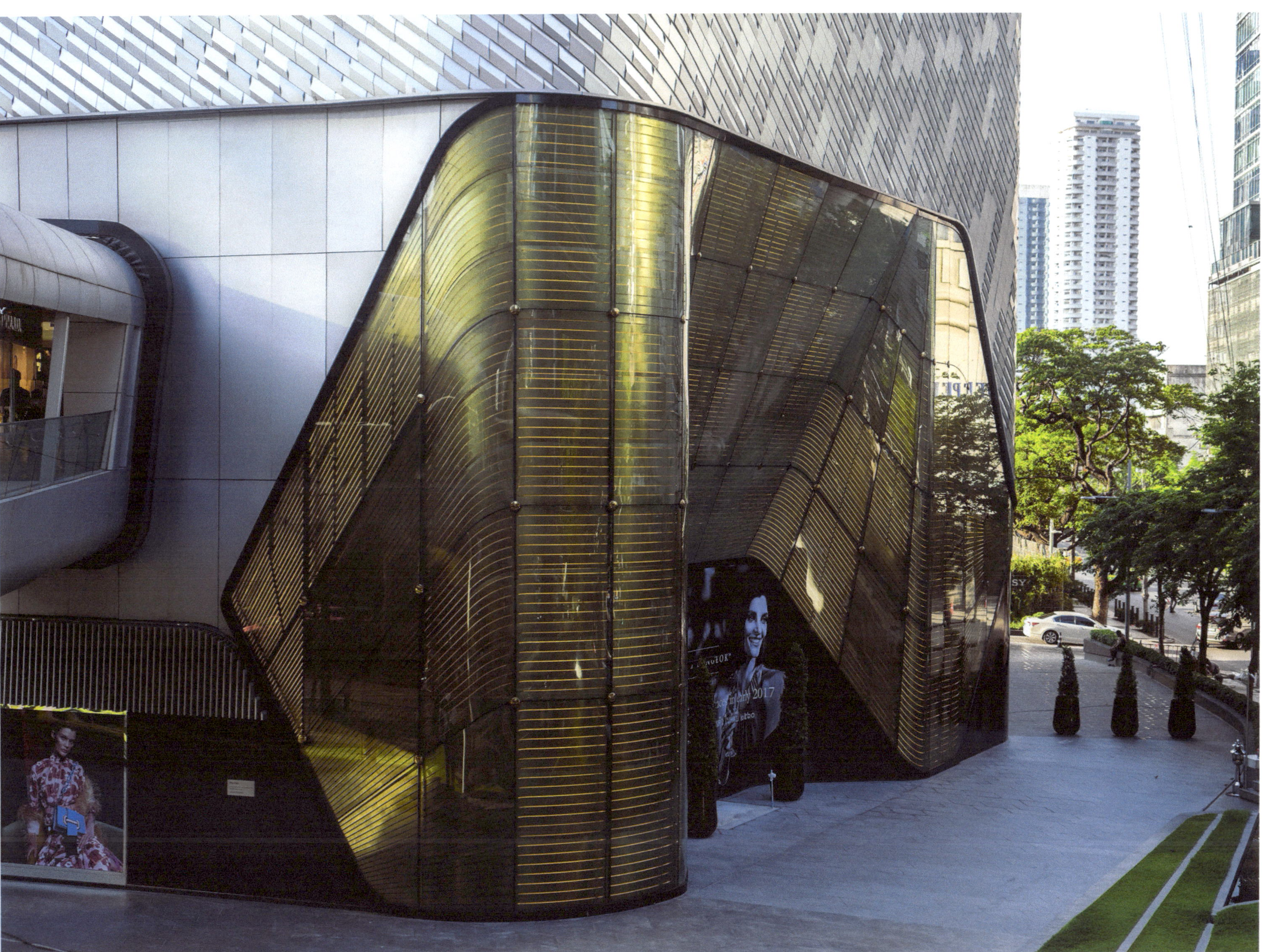

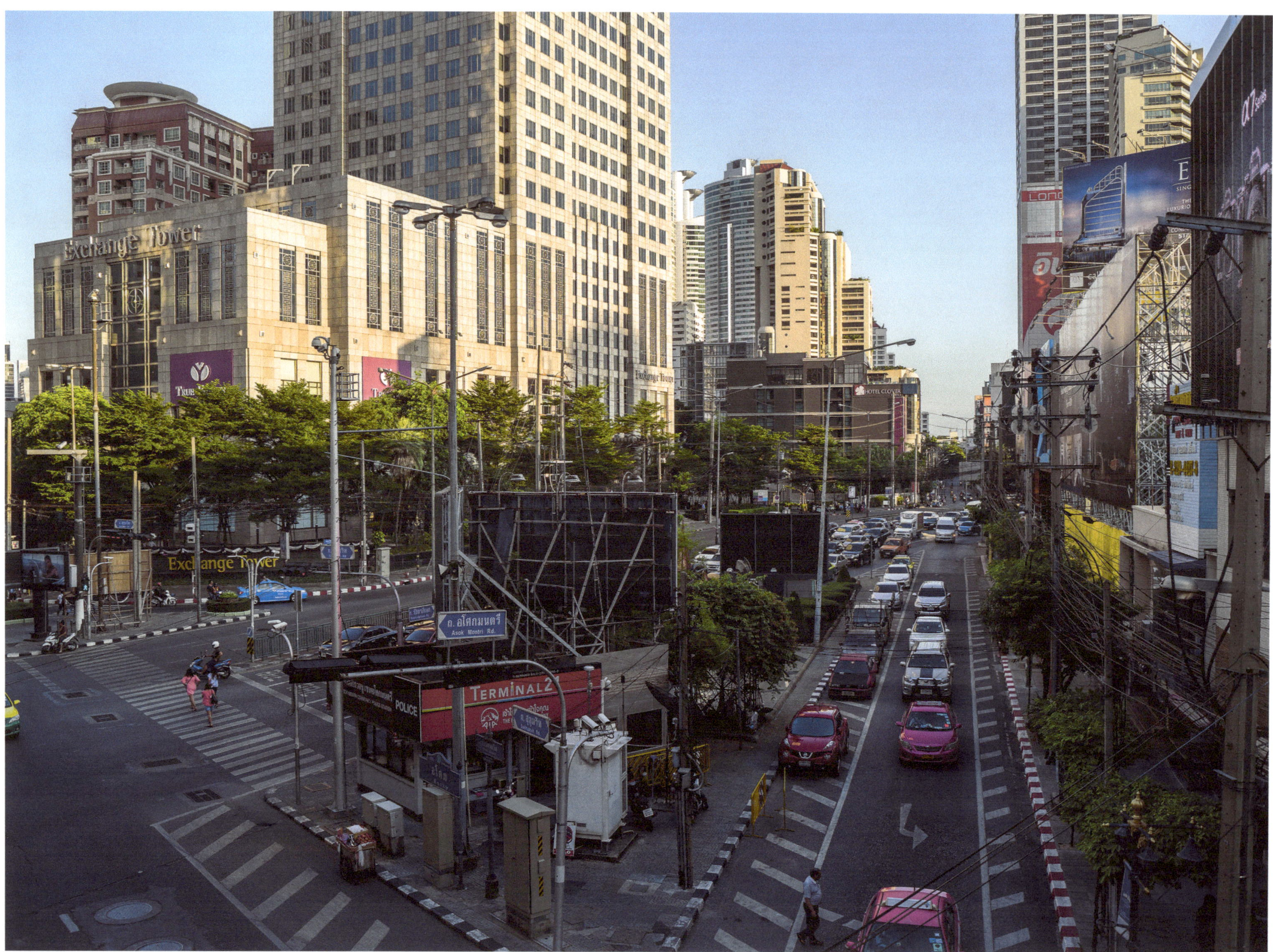

Exchange Tower
Exchange Tower
ถ. อโศกมนตรี
Asok Montri Rd.
TERMINAL21
POLICE

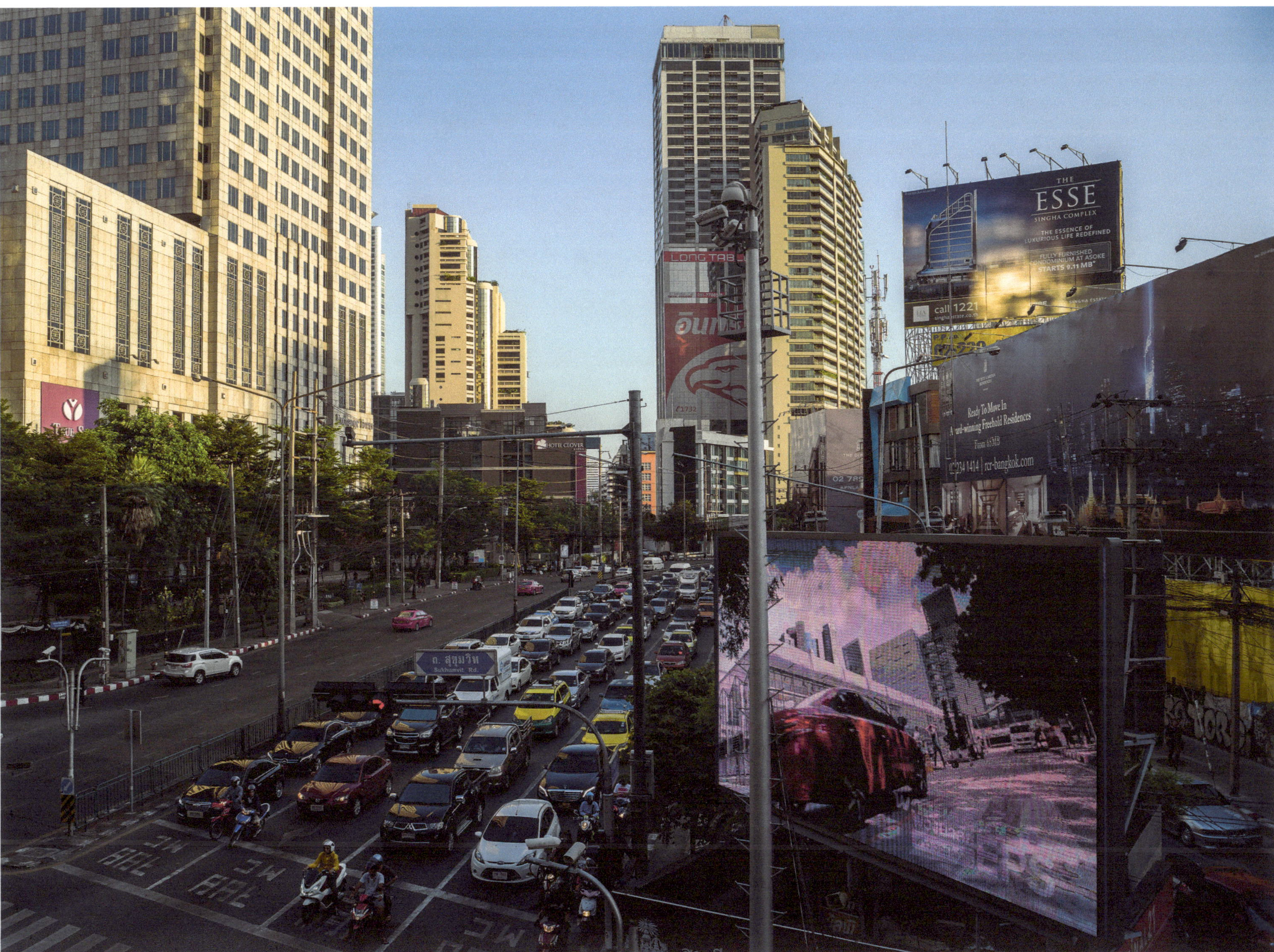
THE
ESSE
SINGHA COMPLEX
THE ESSENCE OF
LUXURIOUS LIFE REDEFINED
FULLY FURNISHED
CONDOMINIUM AT ASOKE
STARTS 9.11 MB*
call 1221
LONG TAB
HOTEL CLOVER
Ready To Move In
Award-winning Freehold Residences
ถ. สุขุมวิท
Sukhumvit Rd.

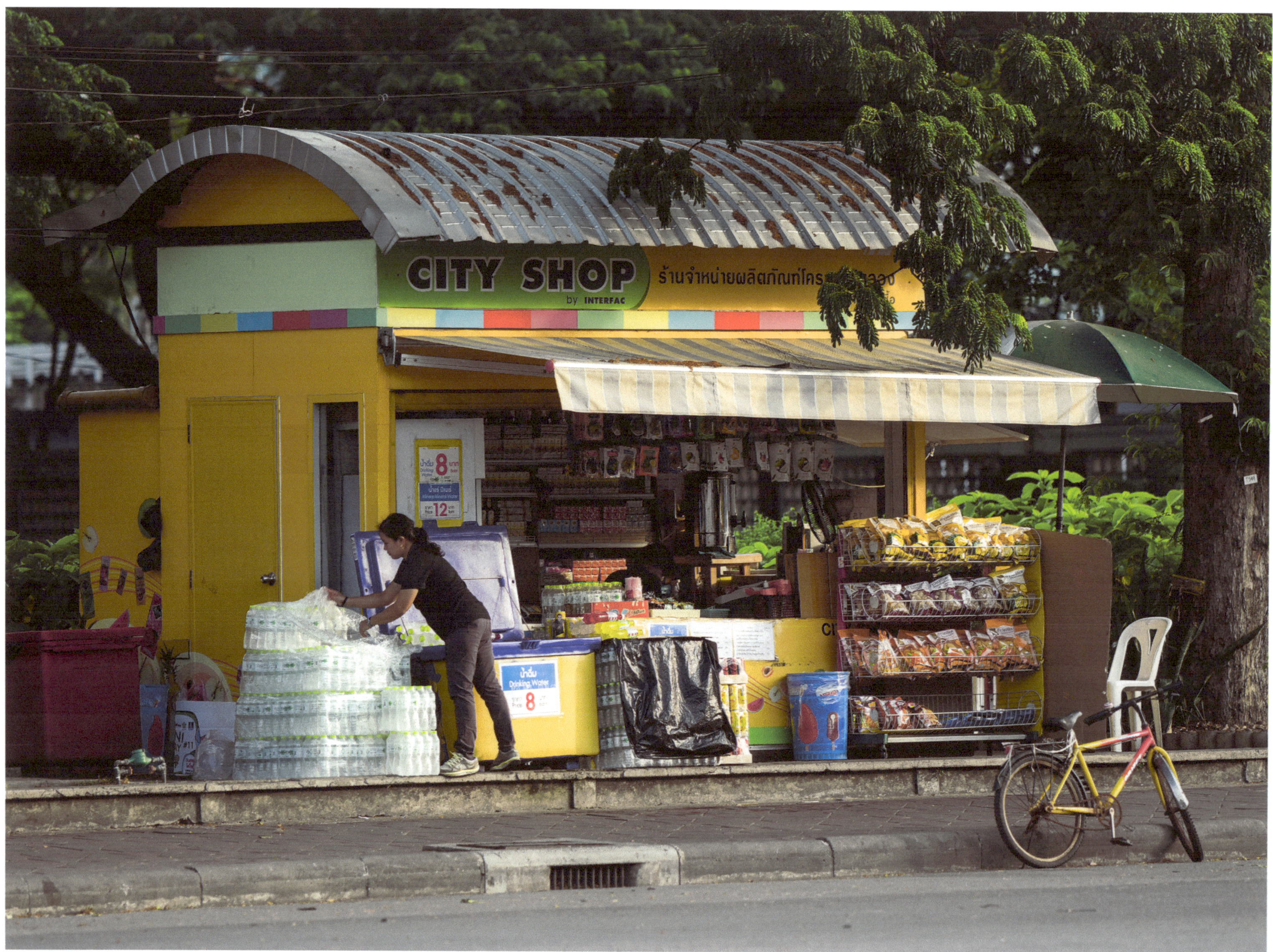
CITY SHOP
by INTERFAC

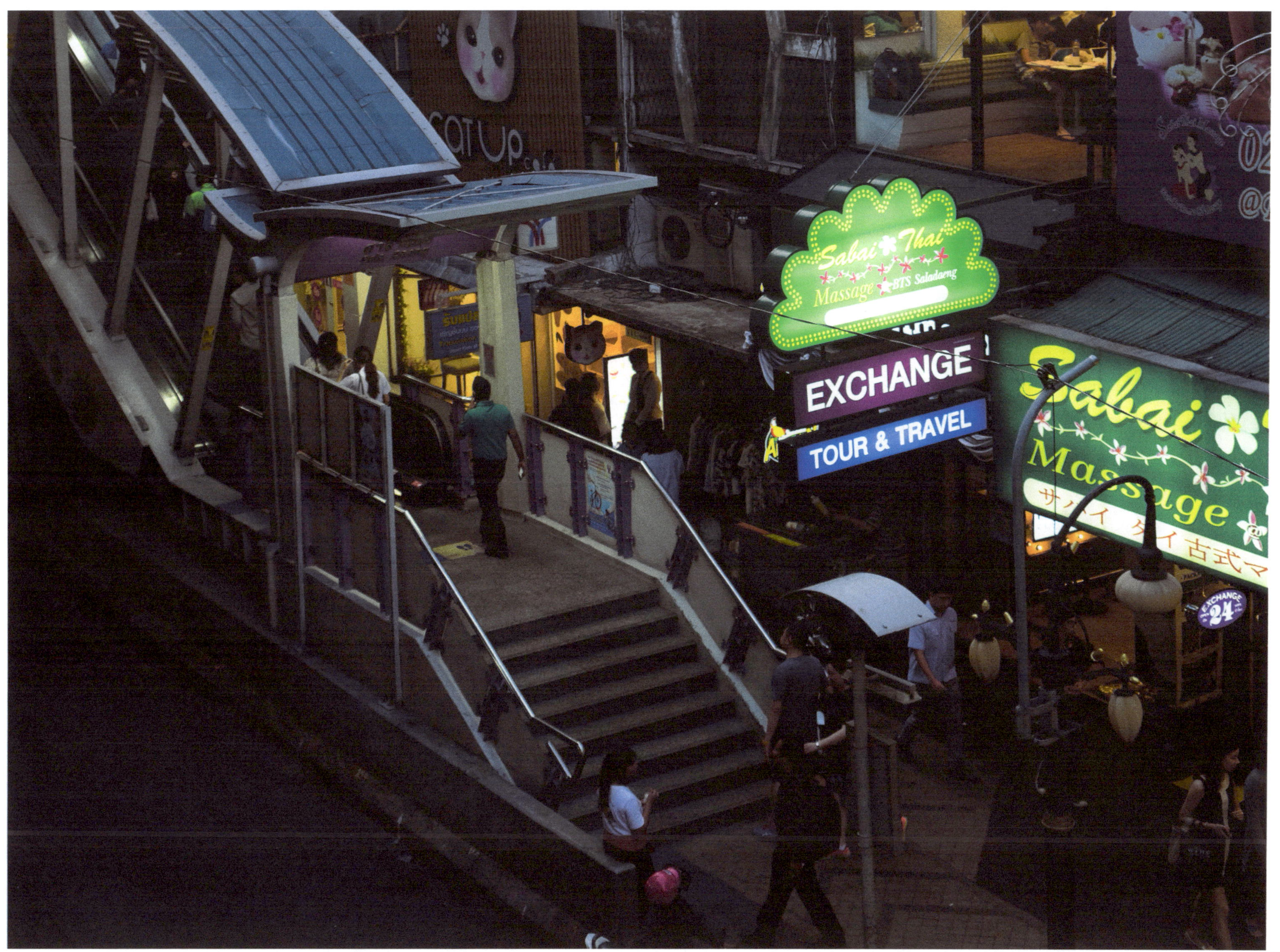
CAT UP
Sabai Thai
Massage BTS Saladaeng
EXCHANGE
TOUR & TRAVEL
Sabai
Massage
サバイ タイ古式マ
EXCHANGE 24

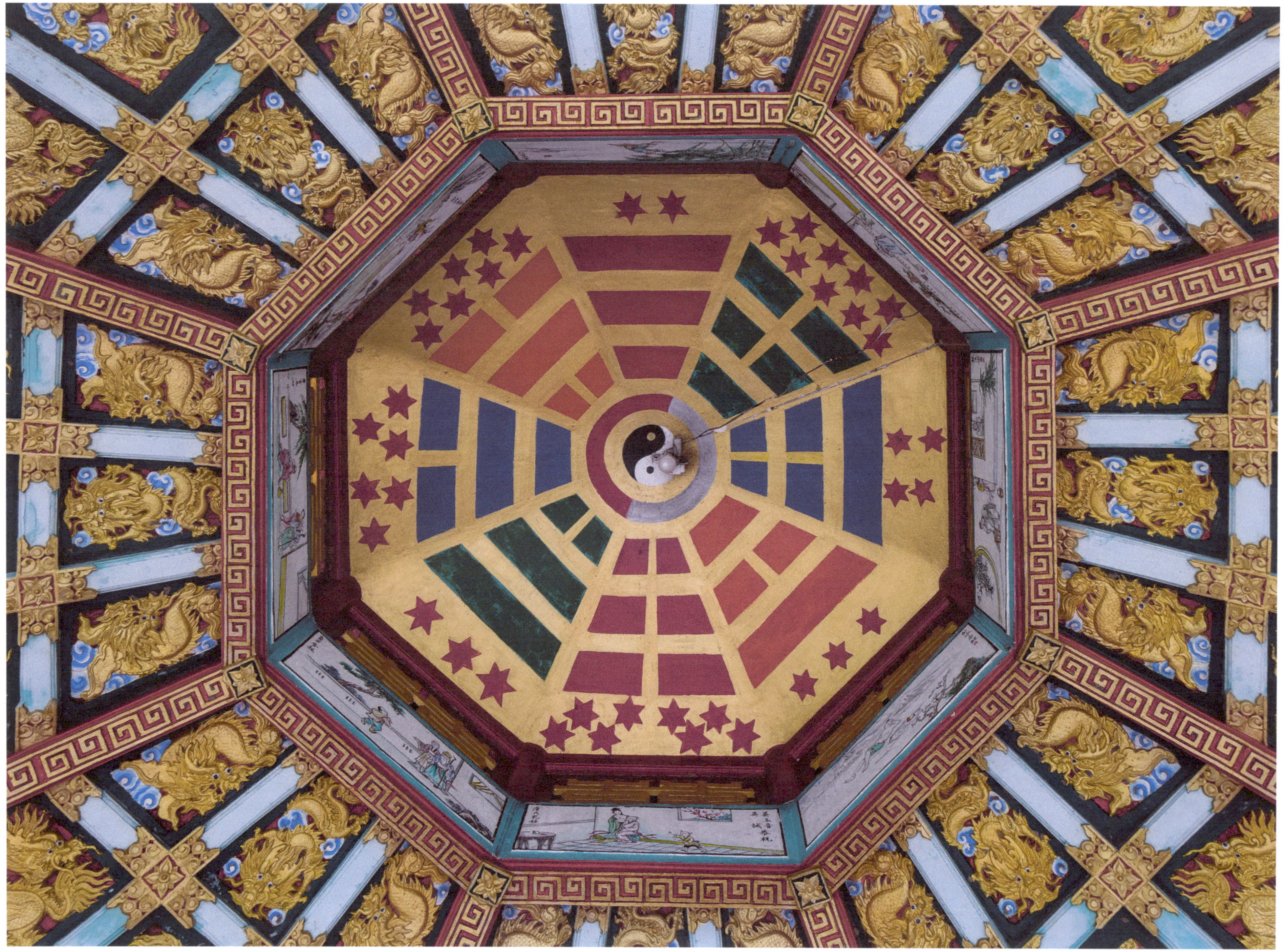

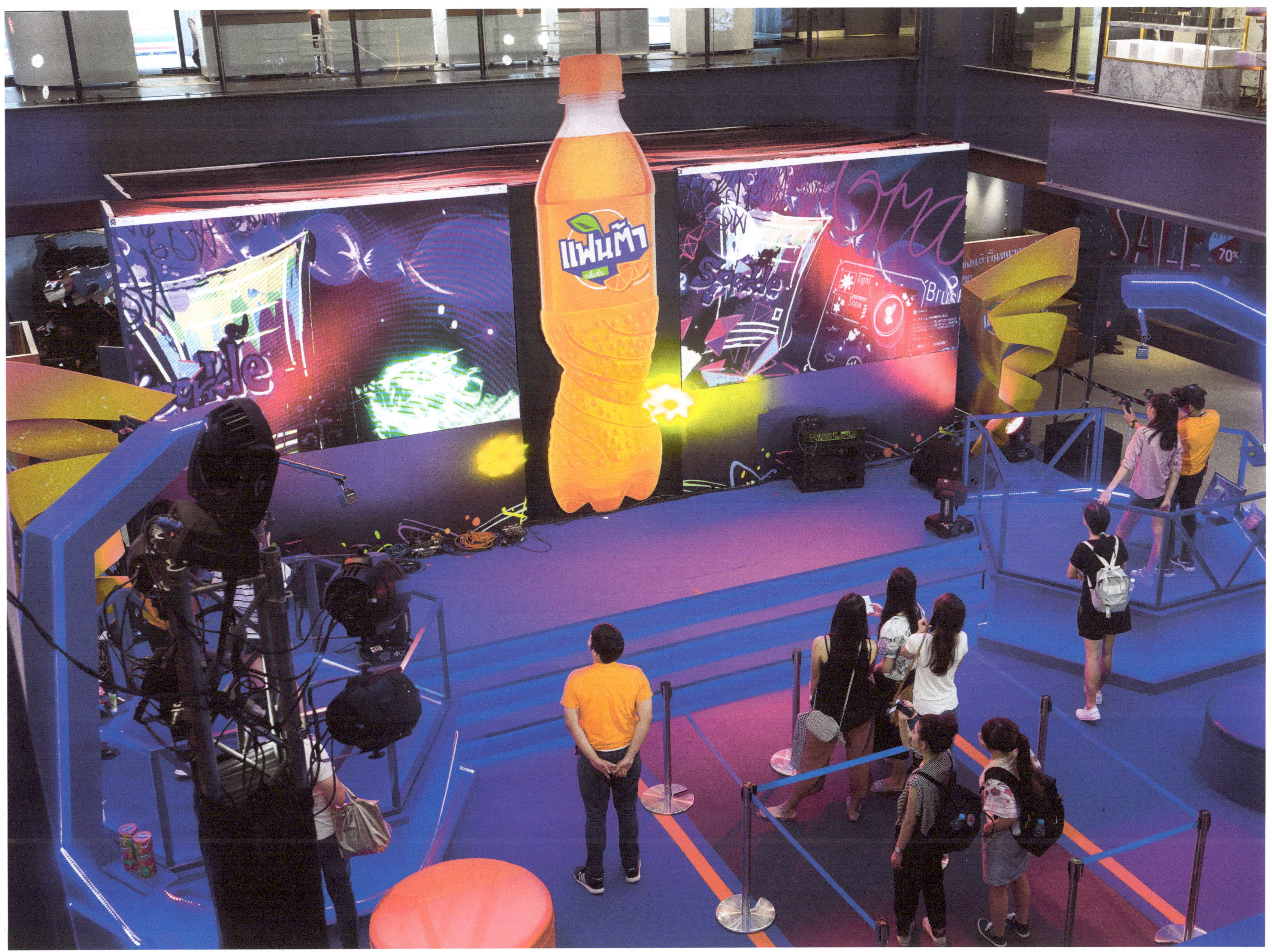
แฟนต้า
SALE
70%

Now! Open

CLOVER
PHARMACY & SOUVENIR

低价

Medicine 药品
Cosmetic 化妆品
Souvenir 纪念品
CLOVER
PHARMACY & SOUVENIR
药店
Logistic 运输
Latex Pillow 乳胶枕
Thai Snacks 泰零食
Bird's Nest 燕窝
最低价
99
低价
所有关于泰国
乳胶枕
零食
药品
燕窝
运输
Natural Rubber Pillow
Patex
Pocky
Longan
PIRATE
CHAMBRE
LOCAL TRATTORIA
SINCE 1997

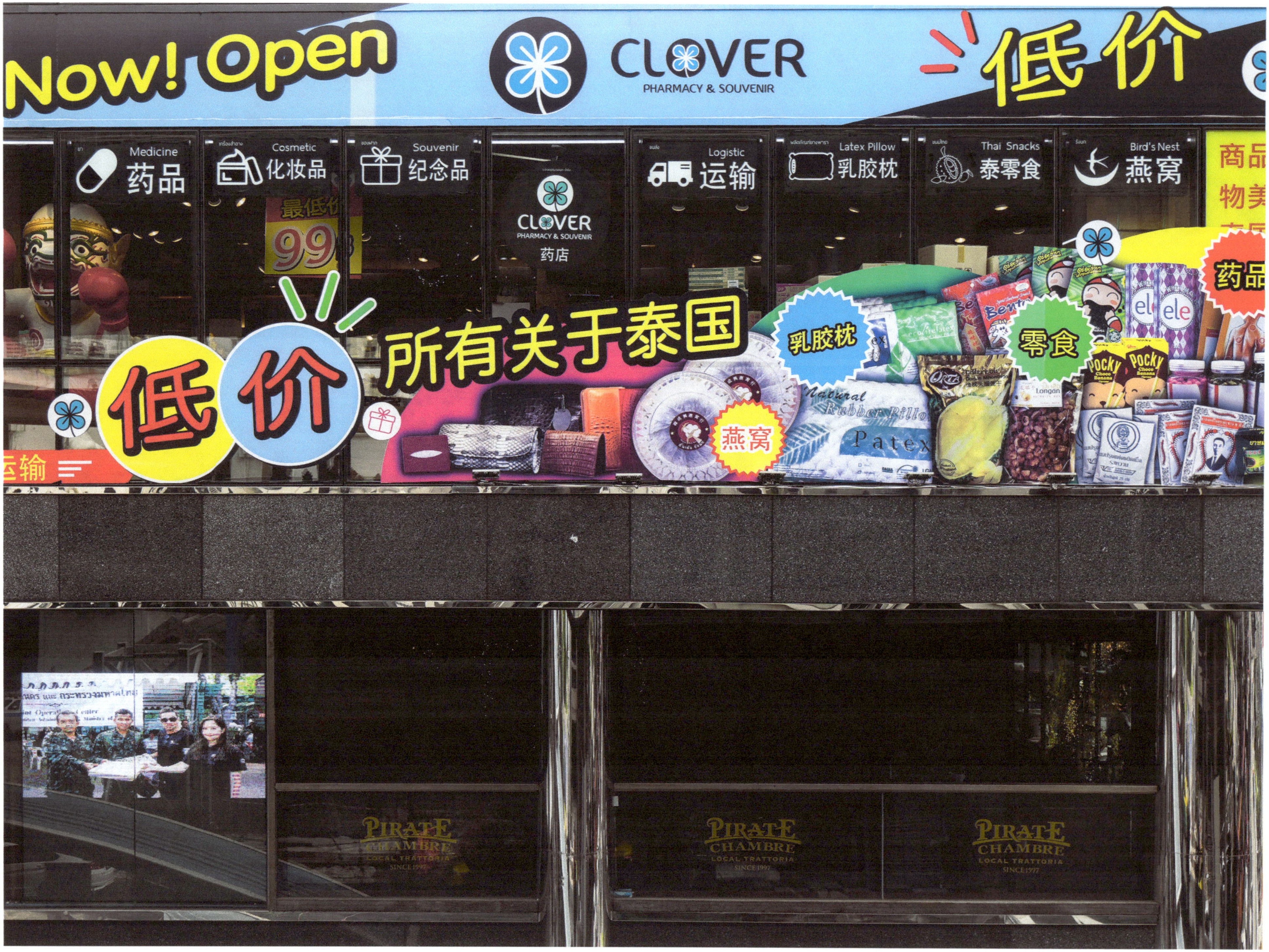

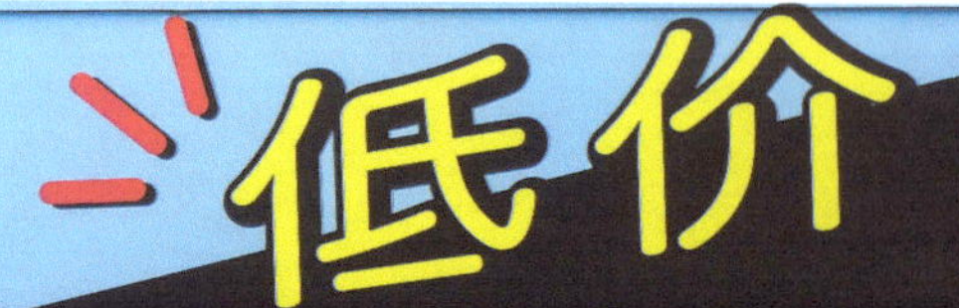

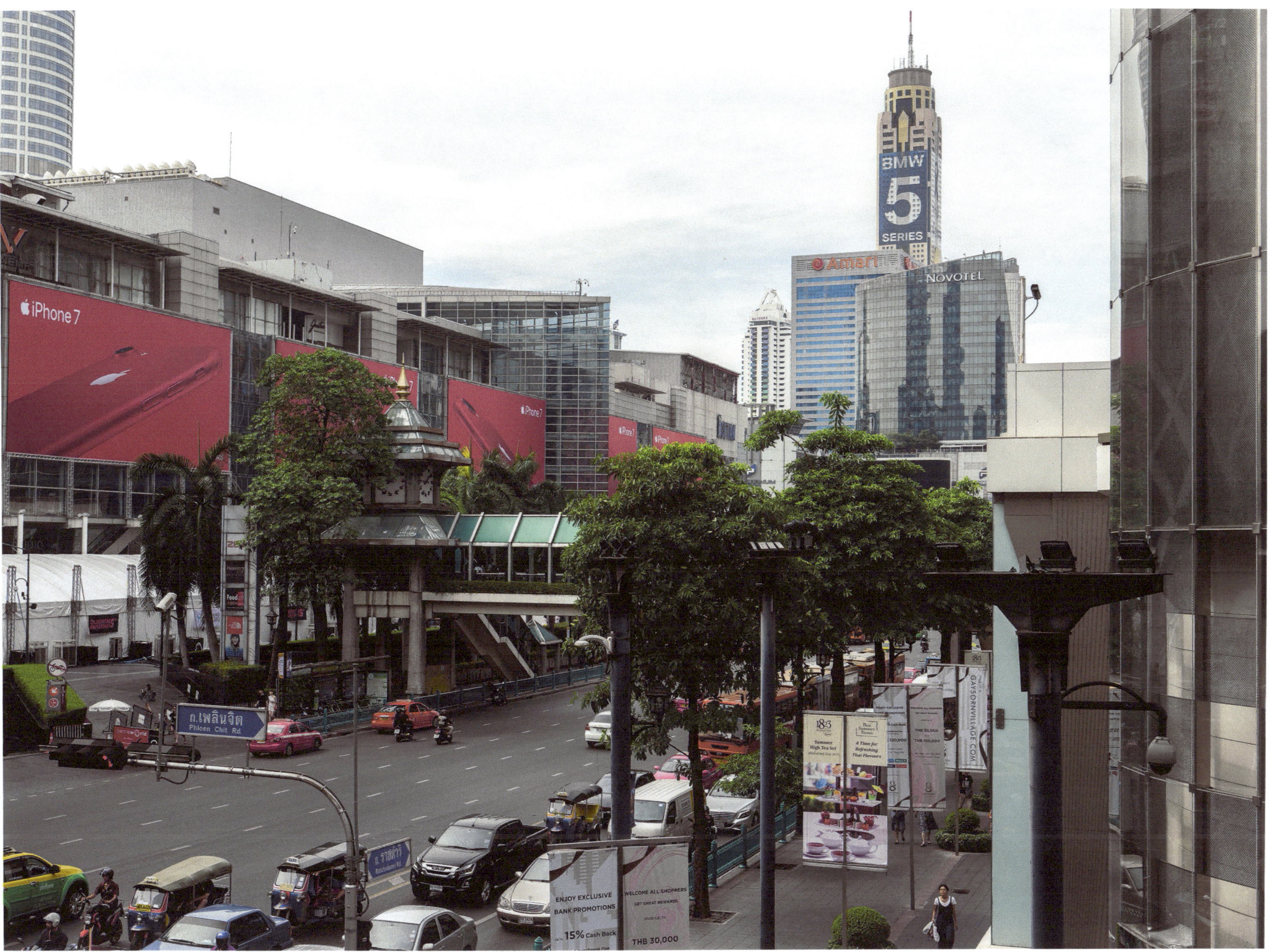
iPhone 7
BMW
5
SERIES
Amari
NOVOTEL
ถ.เพลินจิต
Phloen Chit Rd.
ENJOY EXCLUSIVE
BANK PROMOTIONS
15% Cash Back
WELCOME ALL SHOPPERS
GET GREAT REWARDS
THB 30,000
GAYSORNVILLAGE.COM

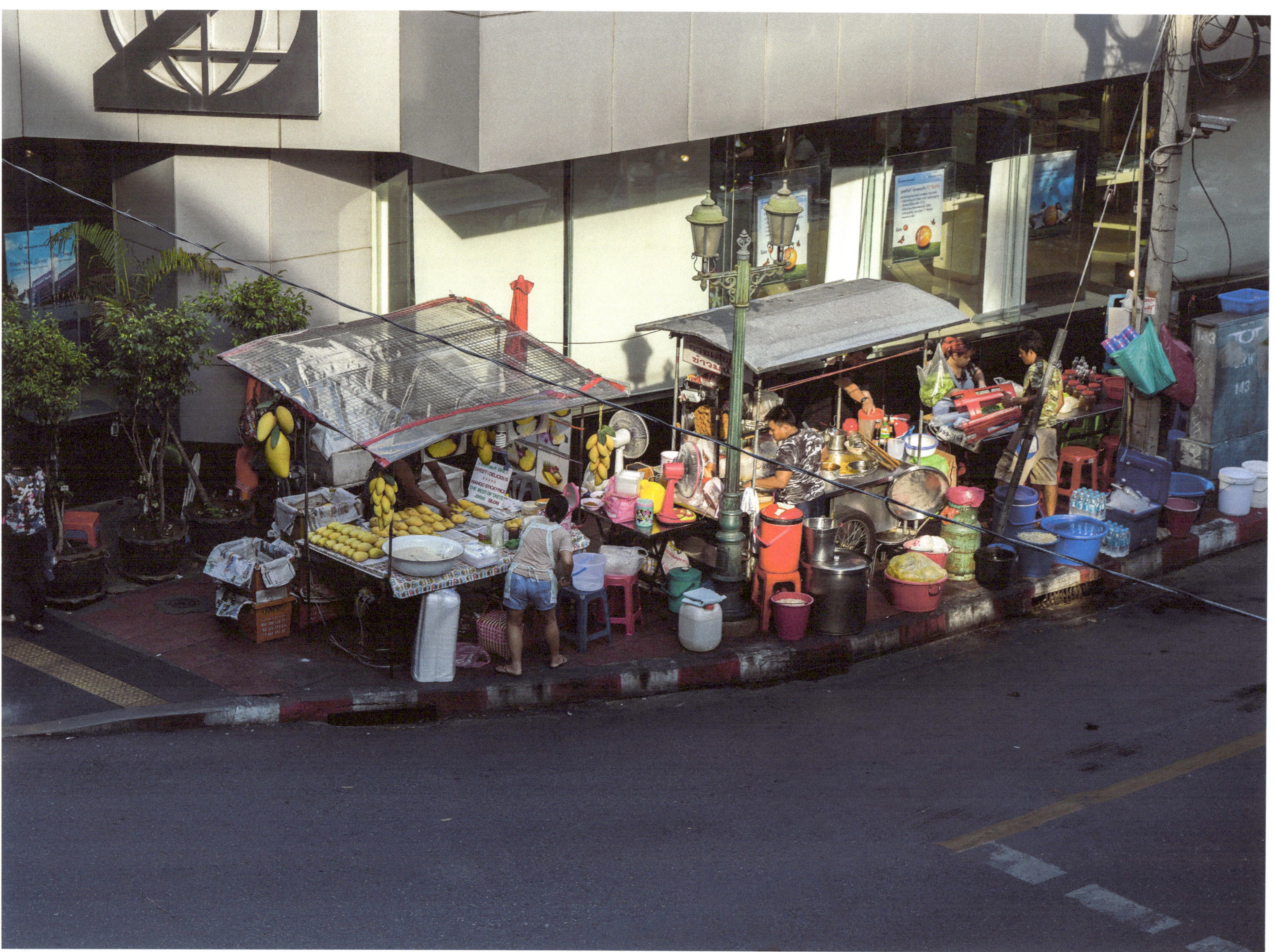
NUMBER ONE
SWEET DELICIOUS
MANGO STICKY RICE
THE BEST OF TASTE
SILOM

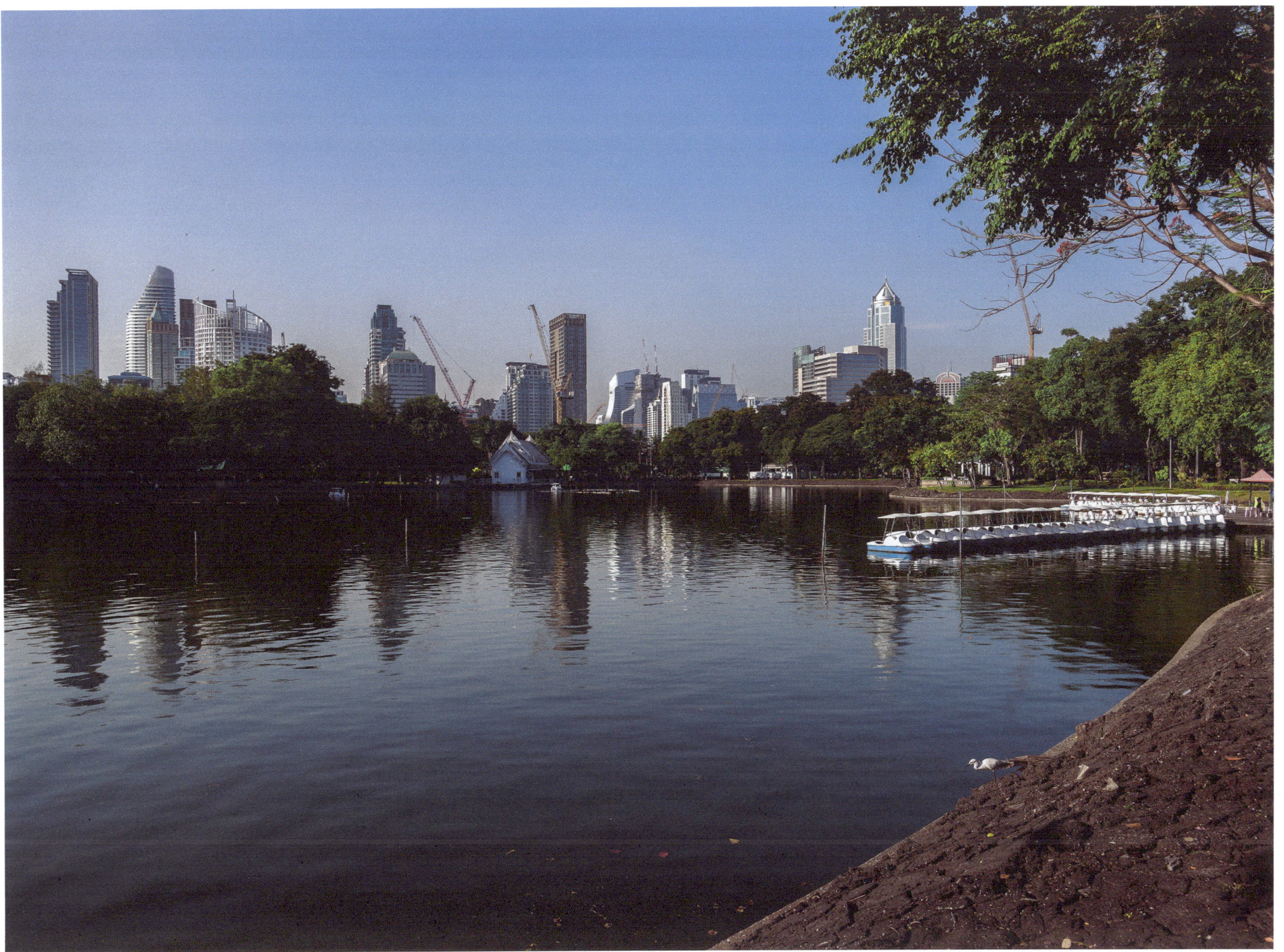

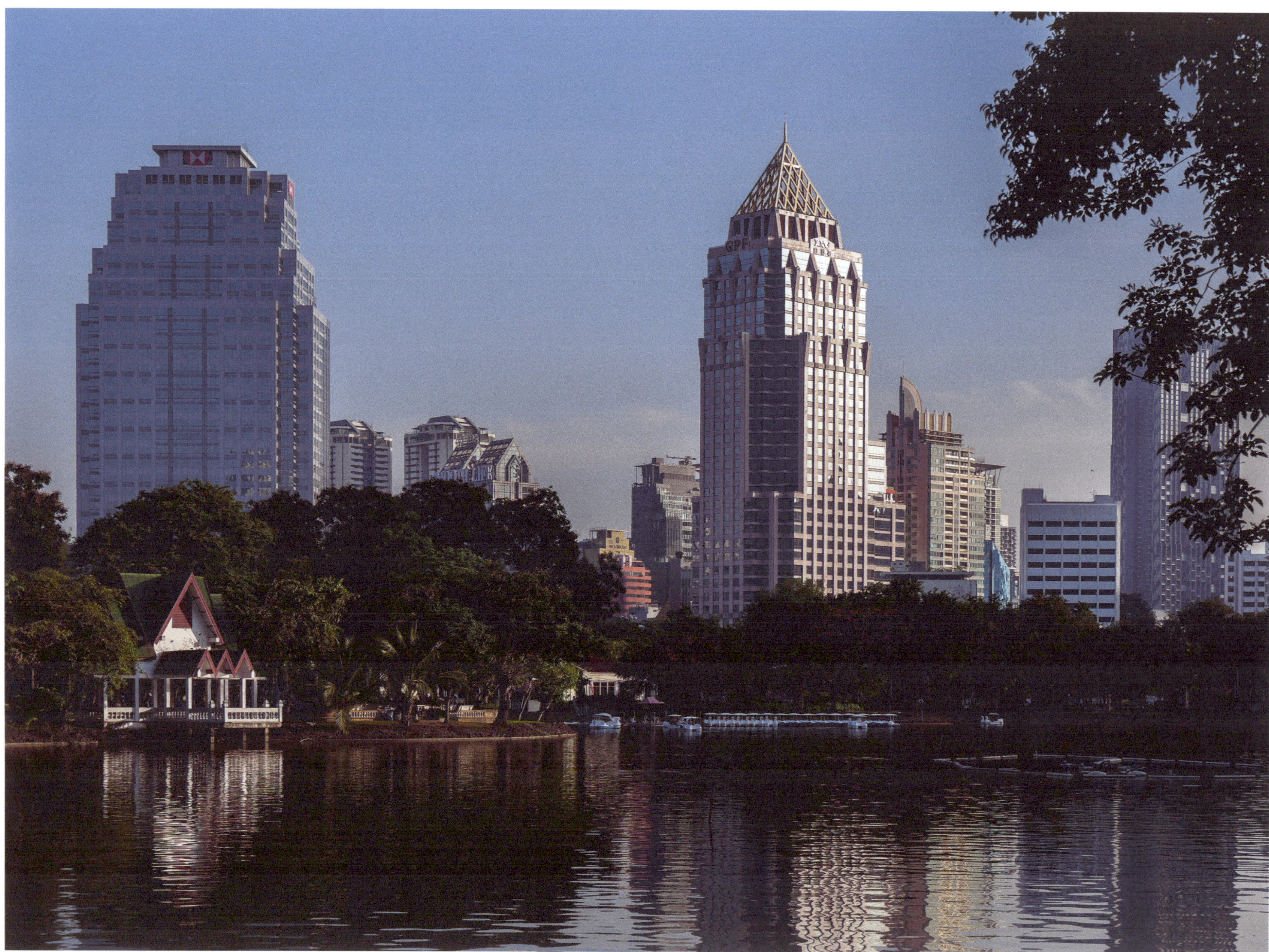

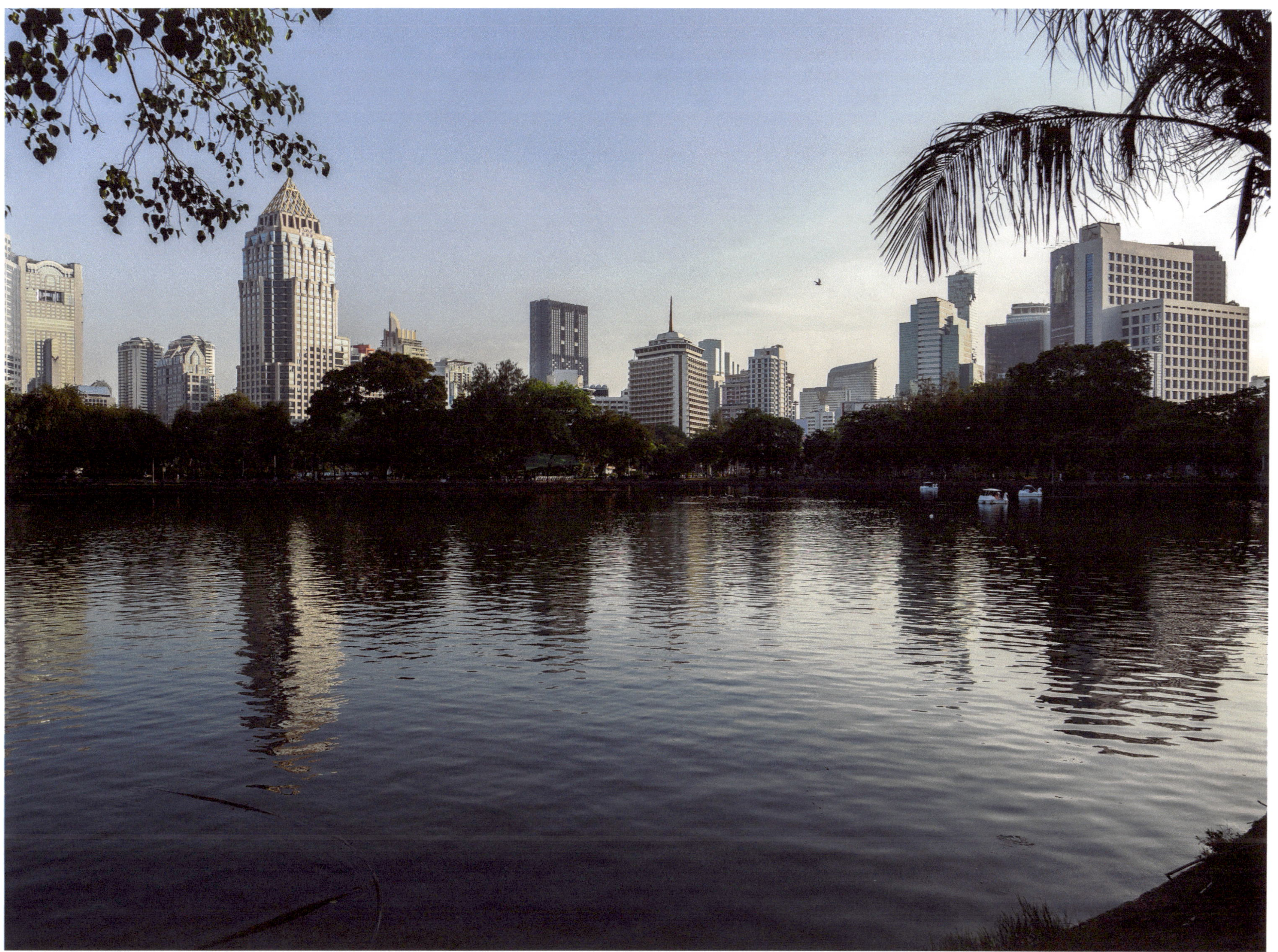

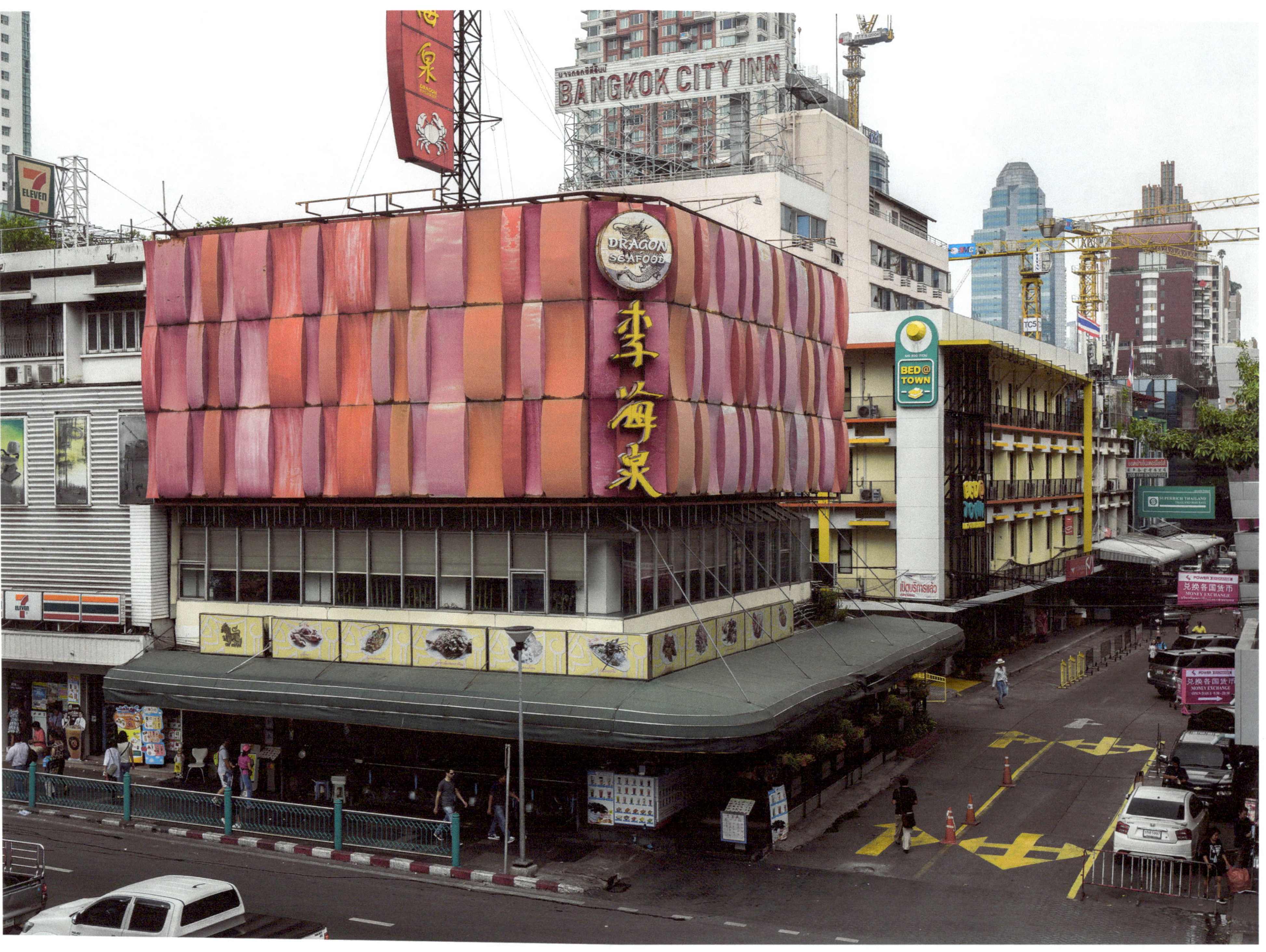

BANGKOK CITY INN
DRAGON SEAFOOD
李海泉
BED@TOWN
MONEY EXCHANGE

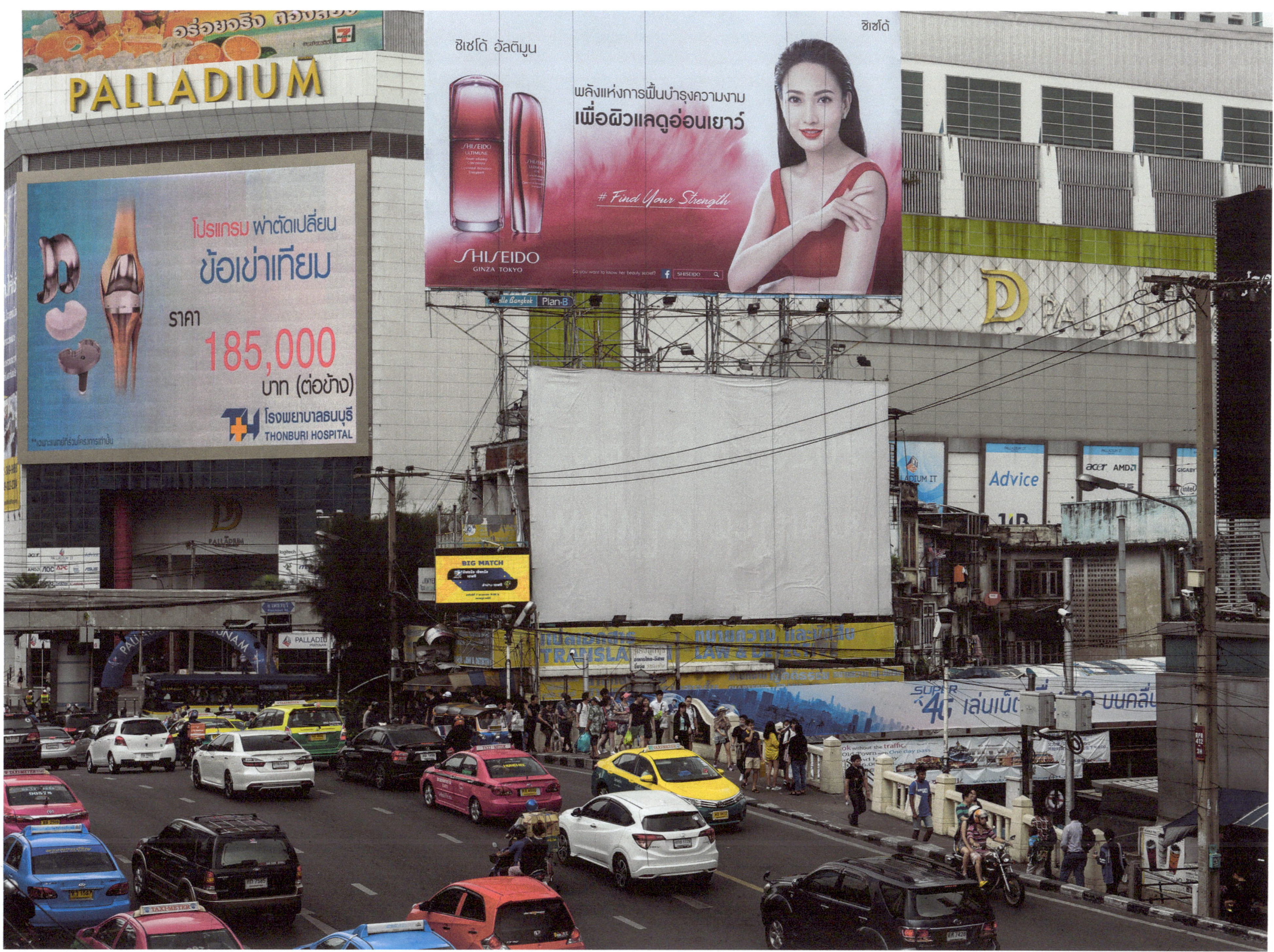
PALLADIUM
โปรแกรม ผ่าตัดเปลี่ยน
ข้อเข่าเทียม
ราคา
185,000
บาท (ต่อข้าง)
โรงพยาบาลธนบุรี
THONBURI HOSPITAL
ชิเซโด้ อัลติมูน
ชิเซโด้
พลังแห่งการฟื้นบำรุงความงาม
เพื่อผิวแลดูอ่อนเยาว์
Find Your Strength
SHISEIDO
GINZA TOKYO
Plan-B
BIG MATCH
Advice
acer AMD
SUPER 4G

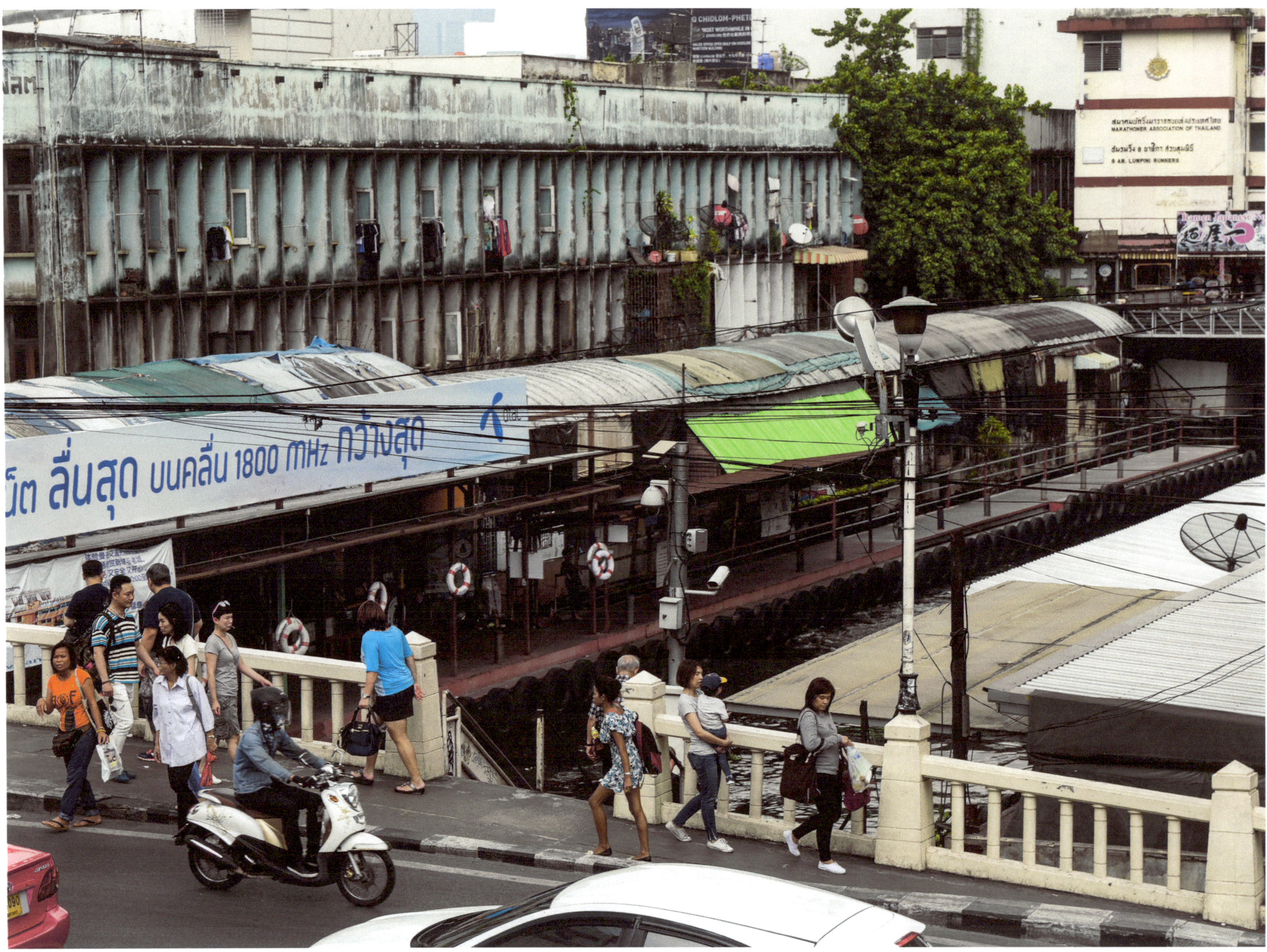
ลื่นสุด บนคลื่น 1800 MHz กว้างสุด
MARATHONER ASSOCIATION OF THAILAND
6 AM. LUMPINI RUNNERS

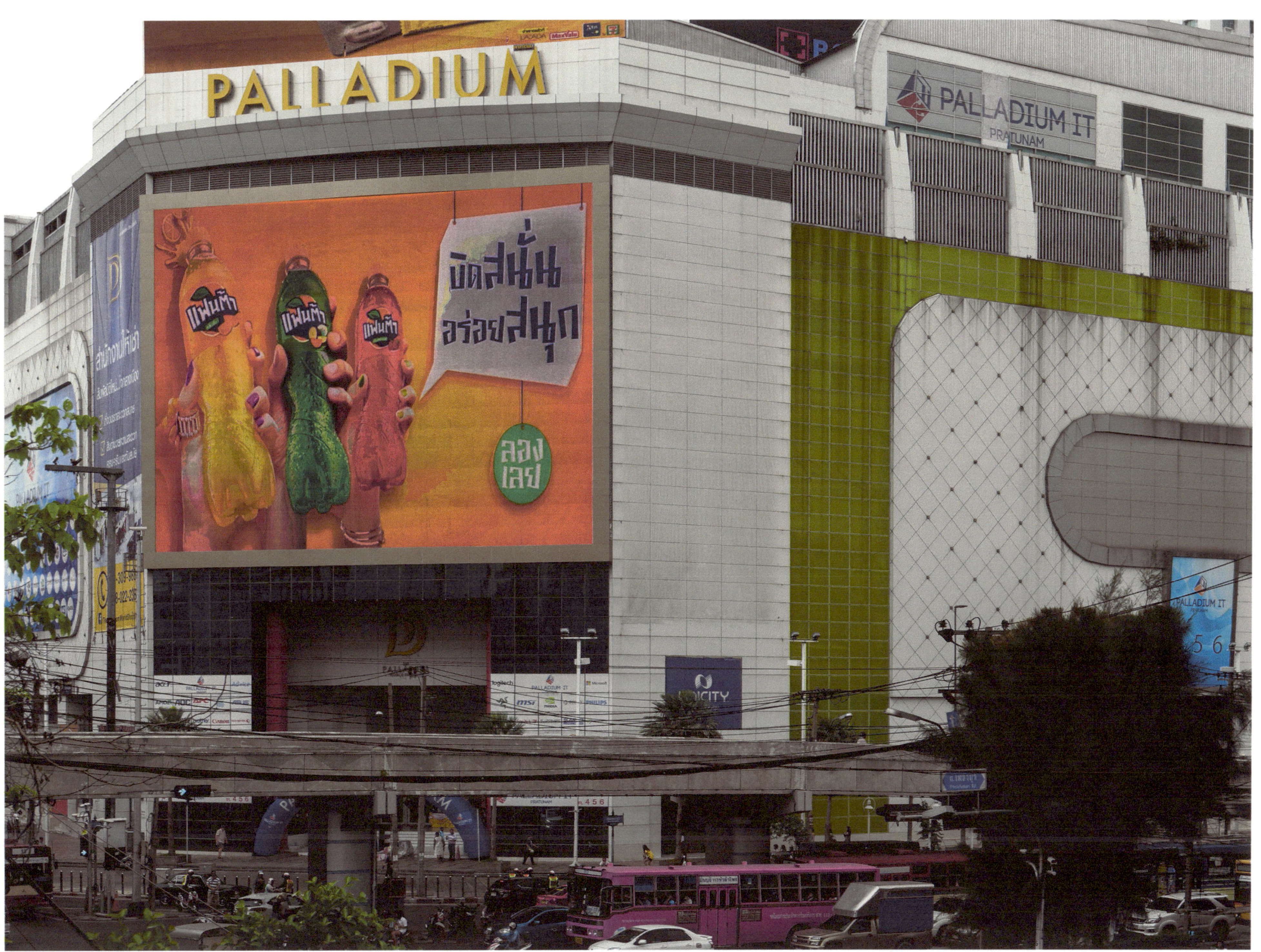
PALLADIUM
PALLADIUM IT
PRATUNAM
บิดสนั่น
อร่อยสนุก
ลอง
เลย
แฟนต้า
PALLADIUM IT

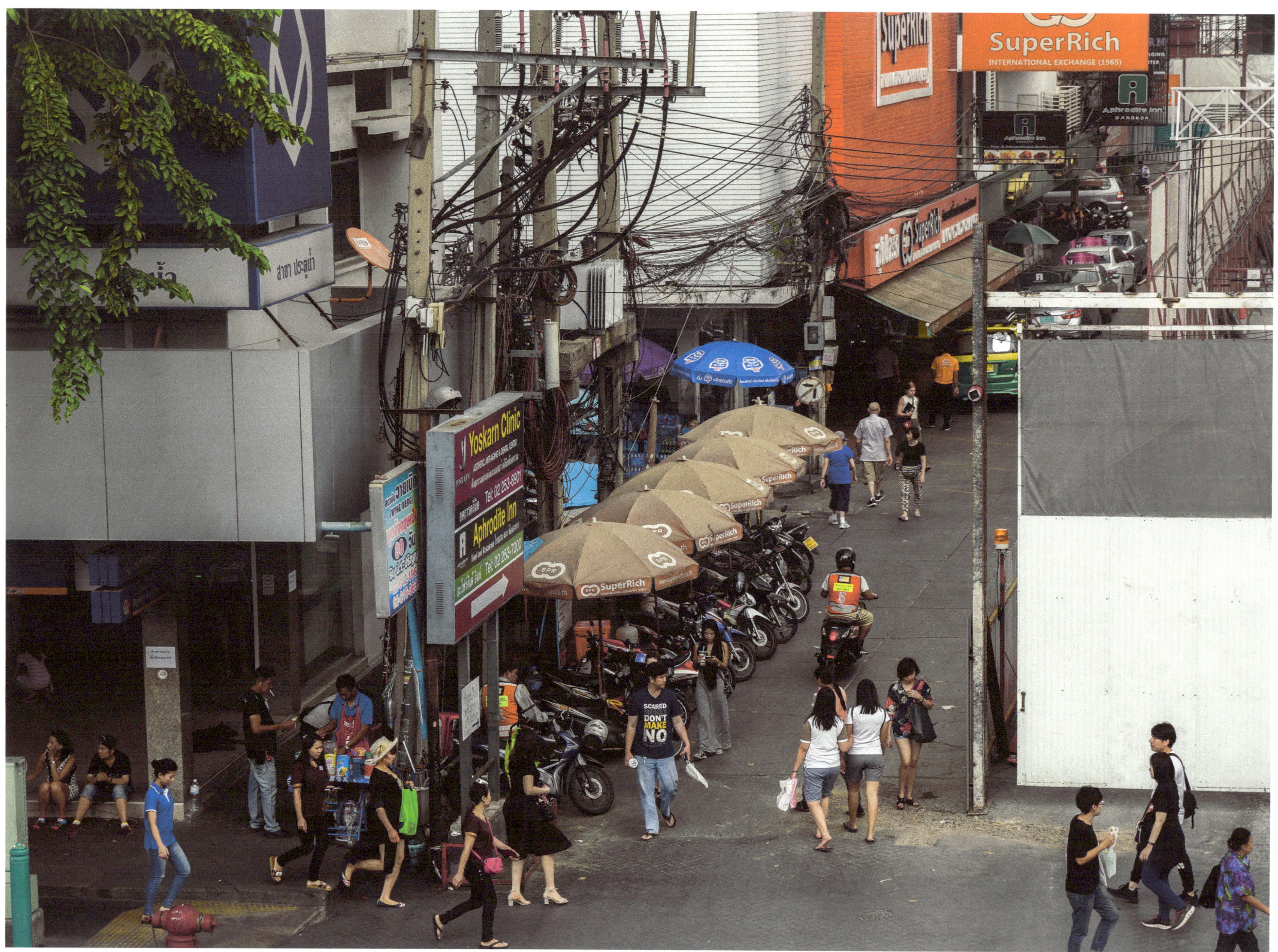
SuperRich
INTERNATIONAL EXCHANGE (1965)
Yoskarn Clinic
Tel: 02 253-8901
Aphrodite Inn
Tel: 02 253-7000
SuperRich
SCARED
DON'T
MAKE
NO

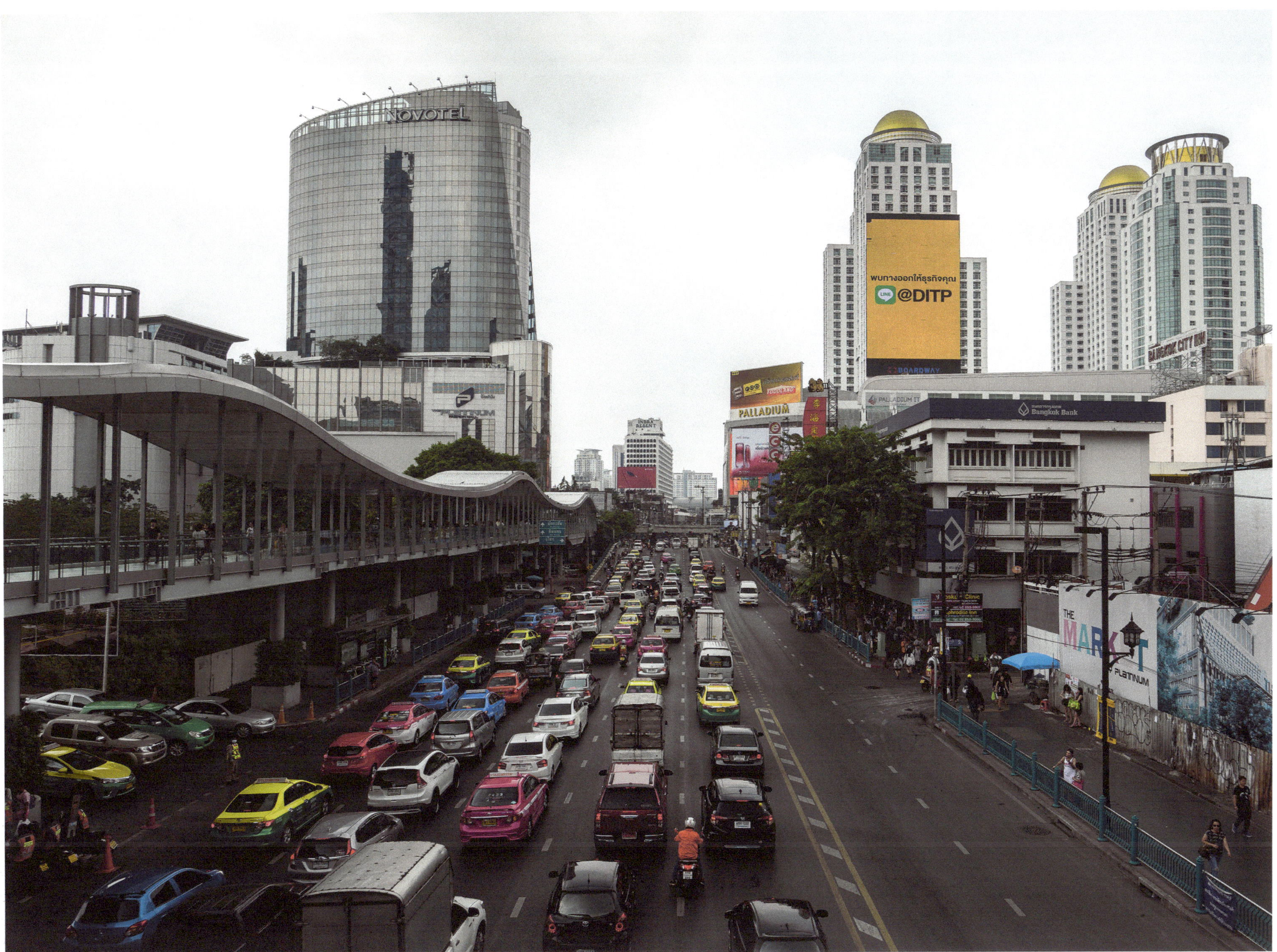
NOVOTEL
พบทางออกให้ธุรกิจคุณ
@DITP
PALLADIUM
Bangkok Bank
THE
PLATINUM

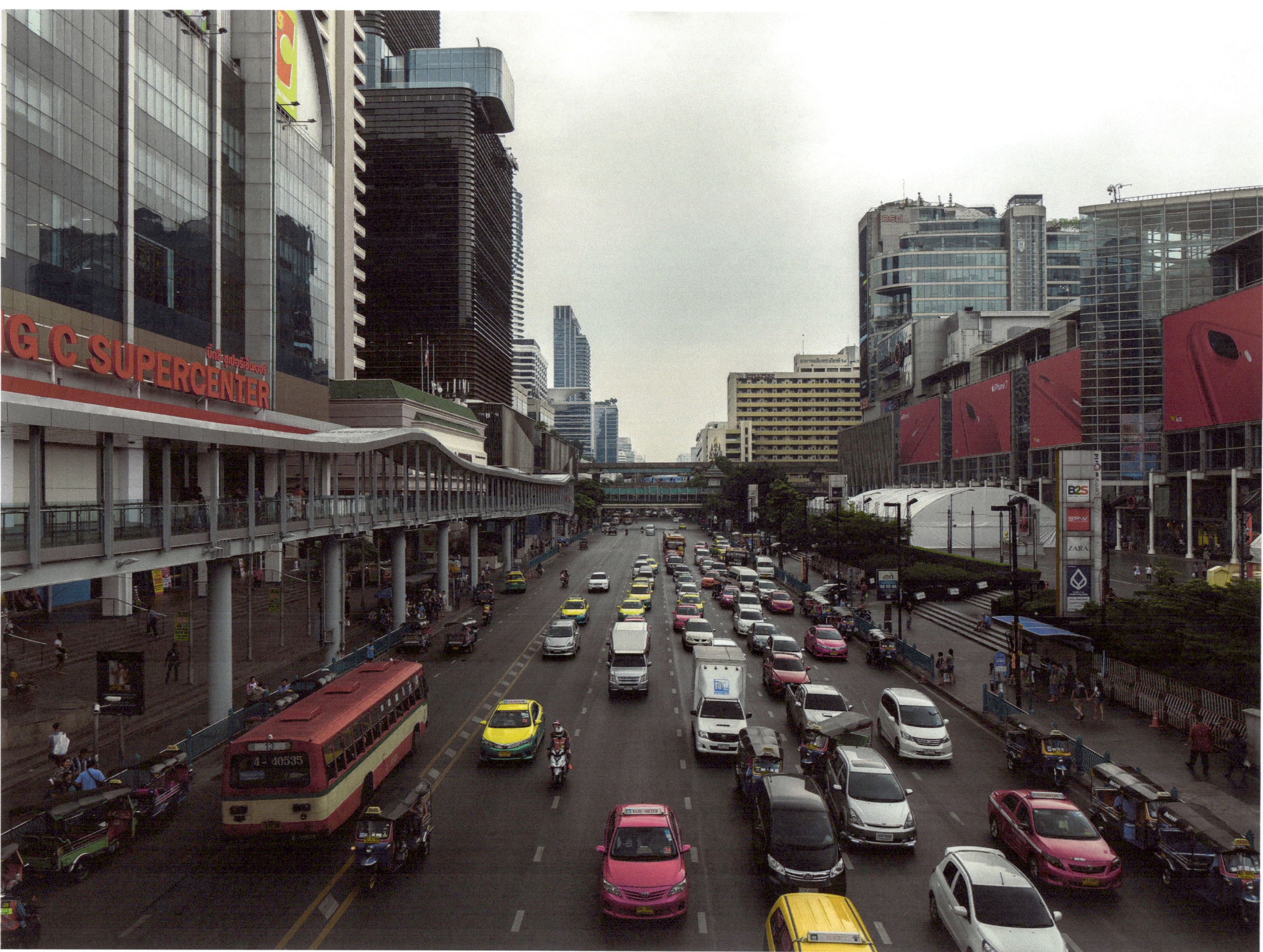
G C SUPERCENTER
13
4- 40535
B2S
ZARA

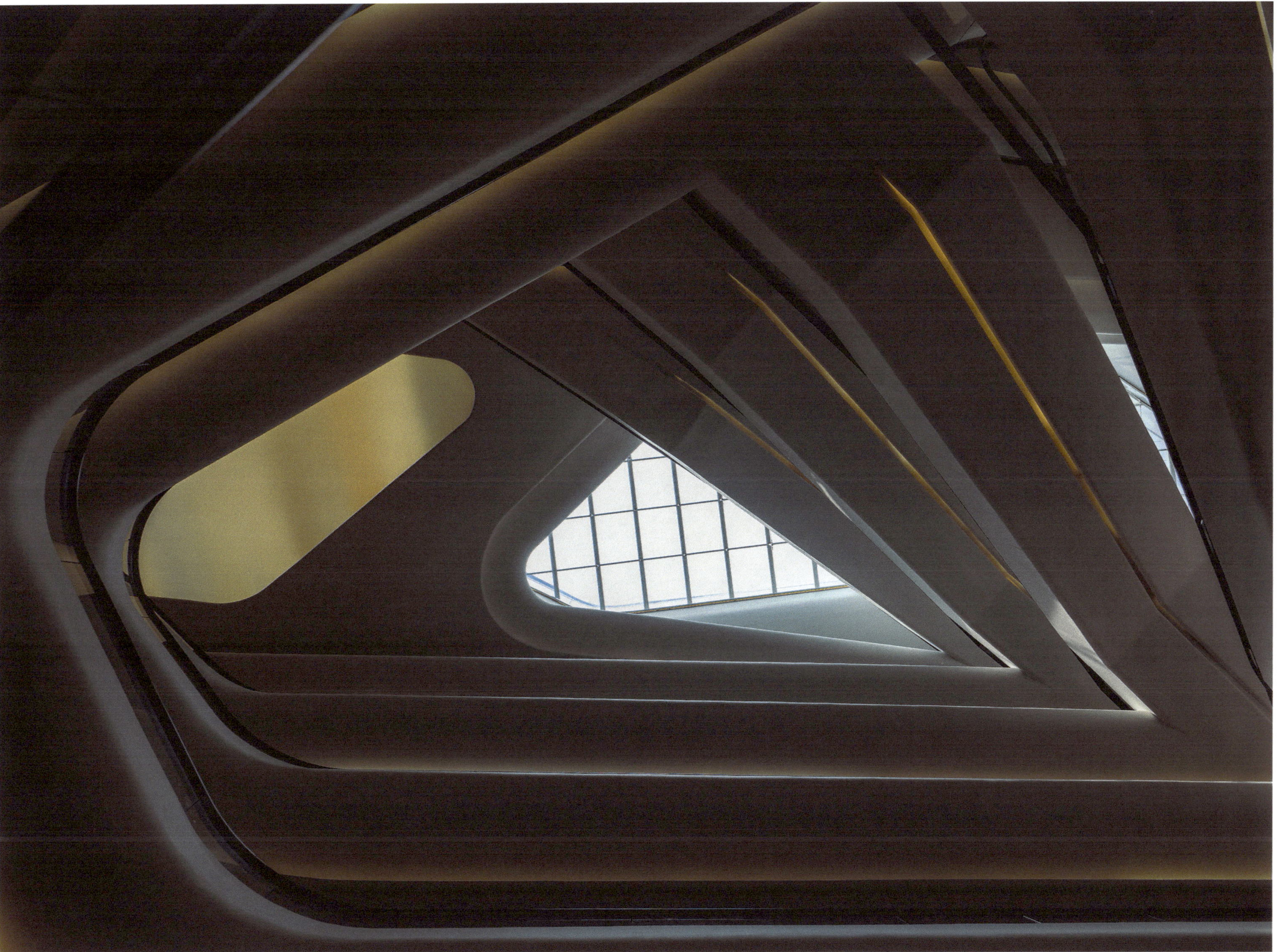

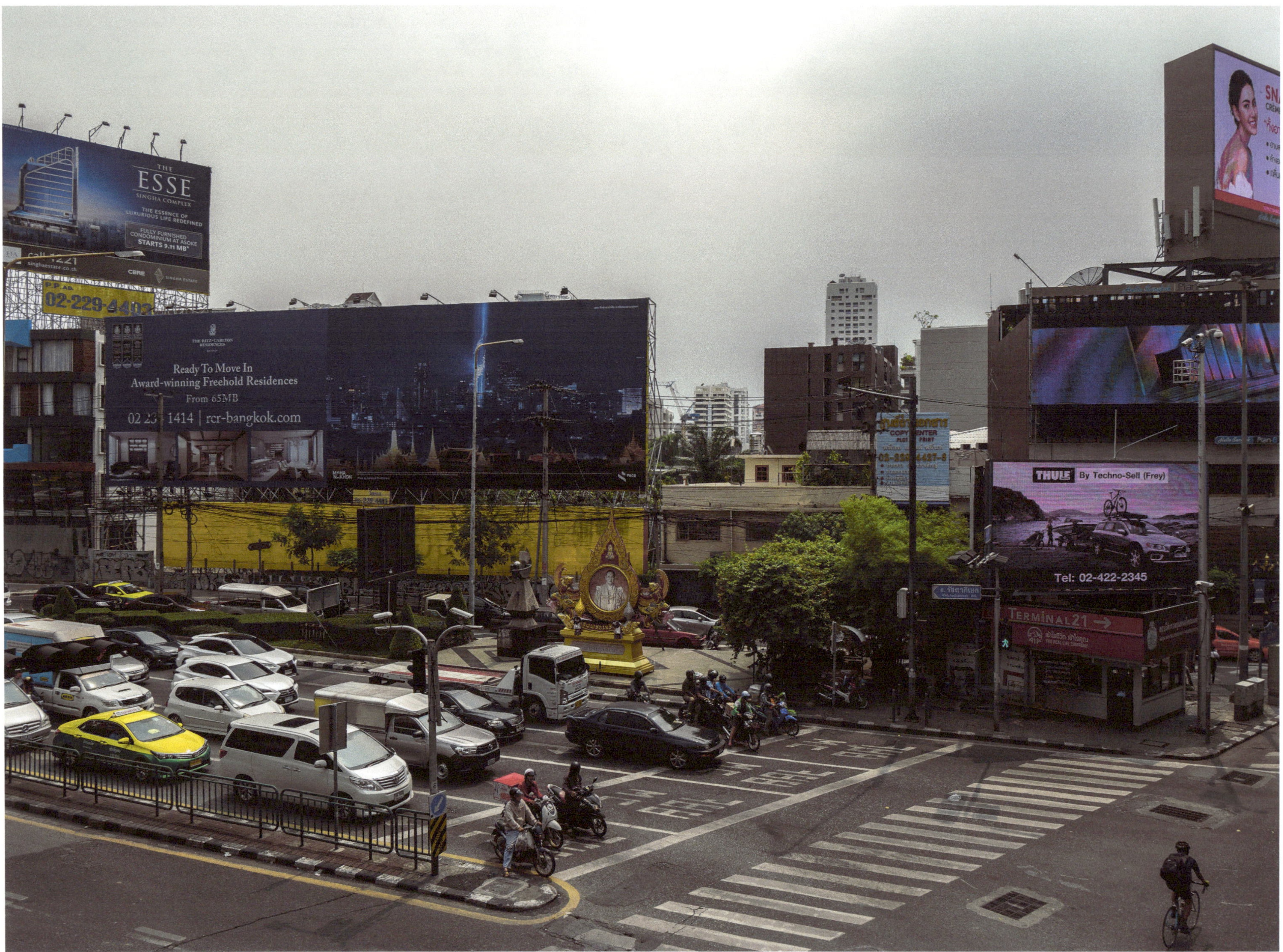
THE
ESSE
SINGHA COMPLEX
THE ESSENCE OF
LUXURIOUS LIFE REDEFINED
FULLY FURNISHED
CONDOMINIUM AT ASOKE
STARTS 9.11 MB*
singhaestate.co.th
CBRE
SINGHA ESTATE
P.P. AD.
THE RITZ-CARLTON
RESIDENCES
Ready To Move In
Award-winning Freehold Residences
From 65MB
1414 | rcr-bangkok.com
THULE By Techno-Sell (Frey)
Tel: 02-422-2345
TERMINAL21
COPY CENTER

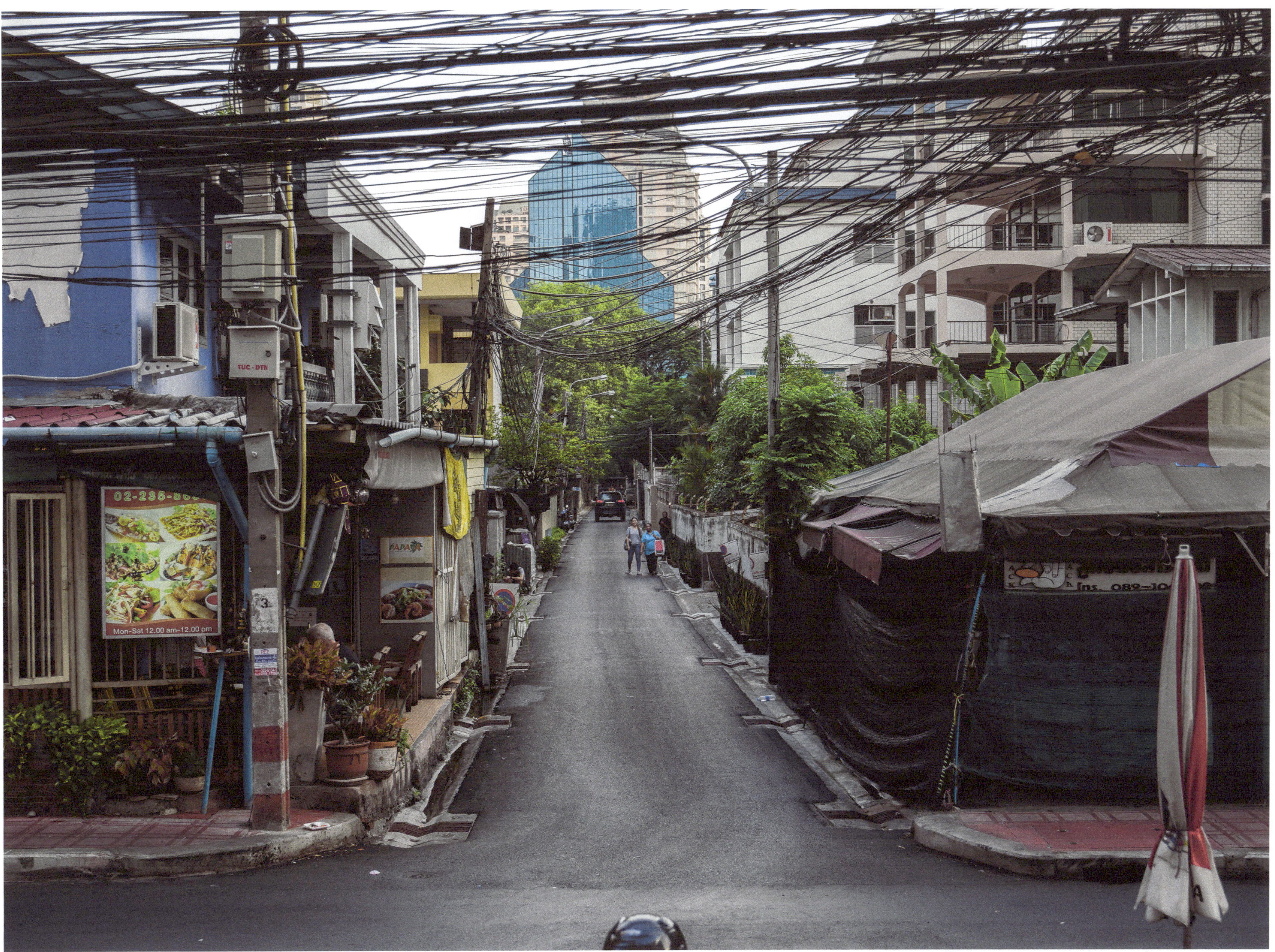
PAPA
Mon-Sat 12.00 am-12.00 pm

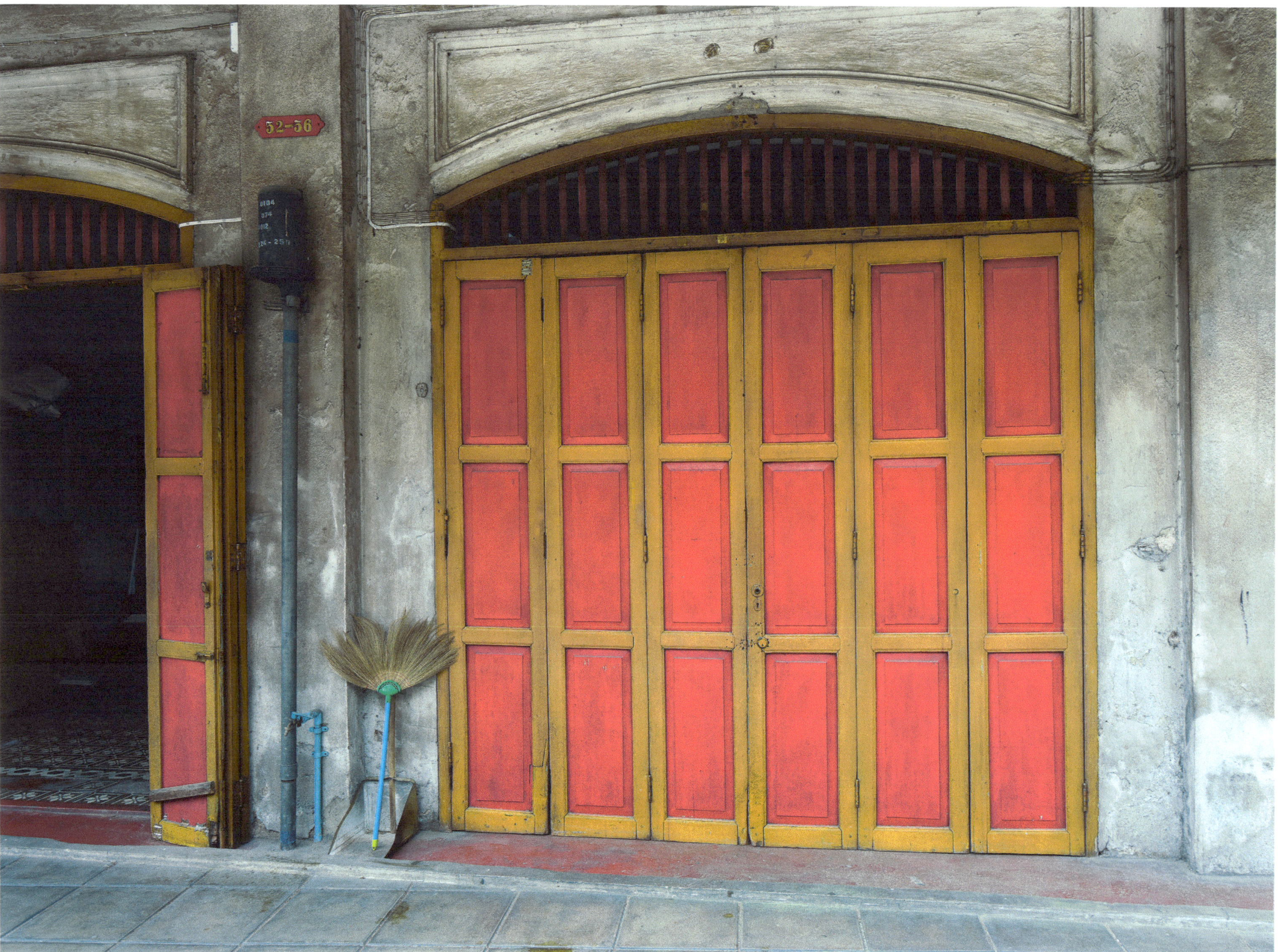
52-56

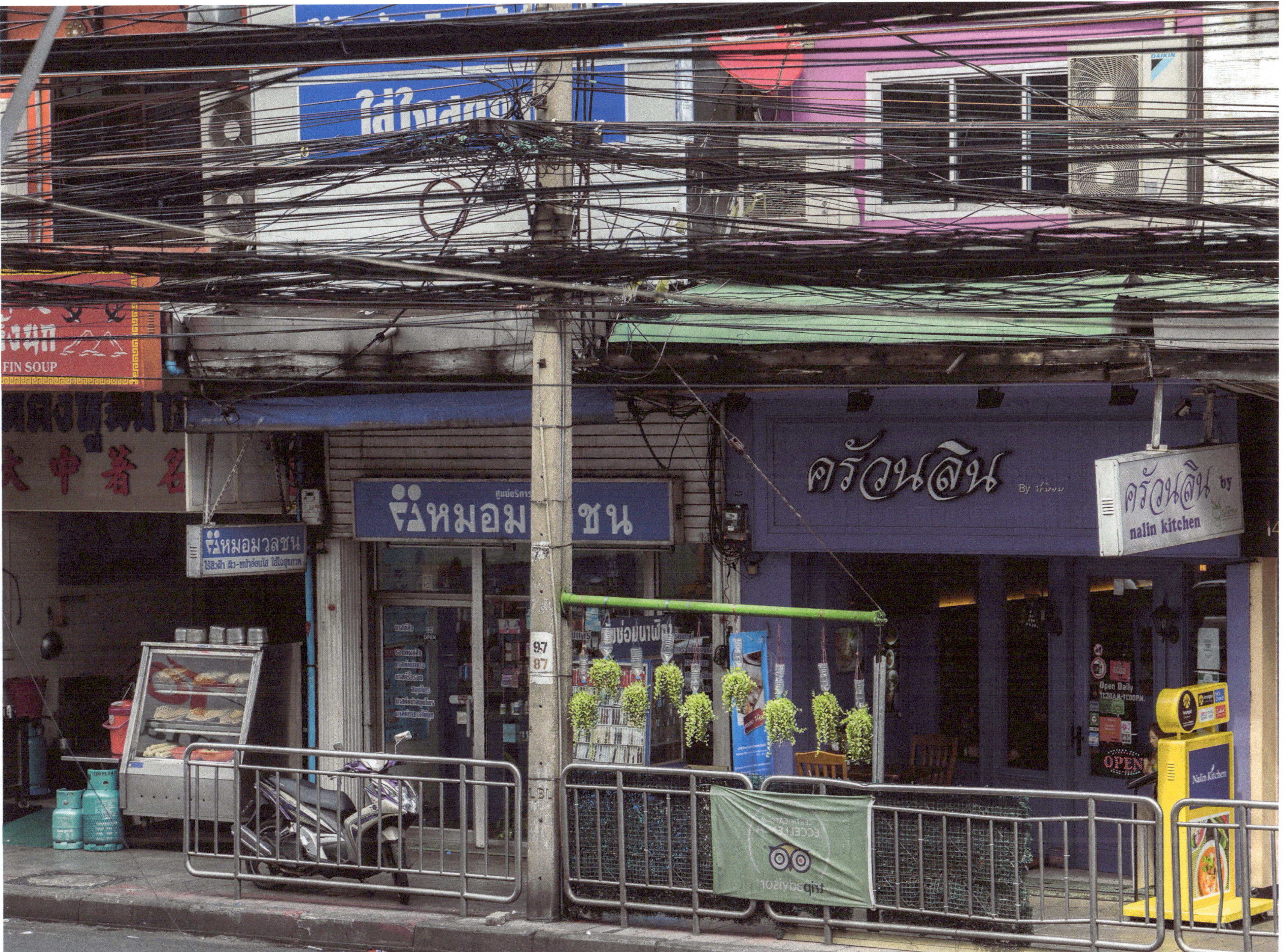

FIN SOUP
หมอมวลชน
ครัวนลิน
ครัวนลิน by
nalin kitchen
Open Daily
OPEN
Nalin Kitchen

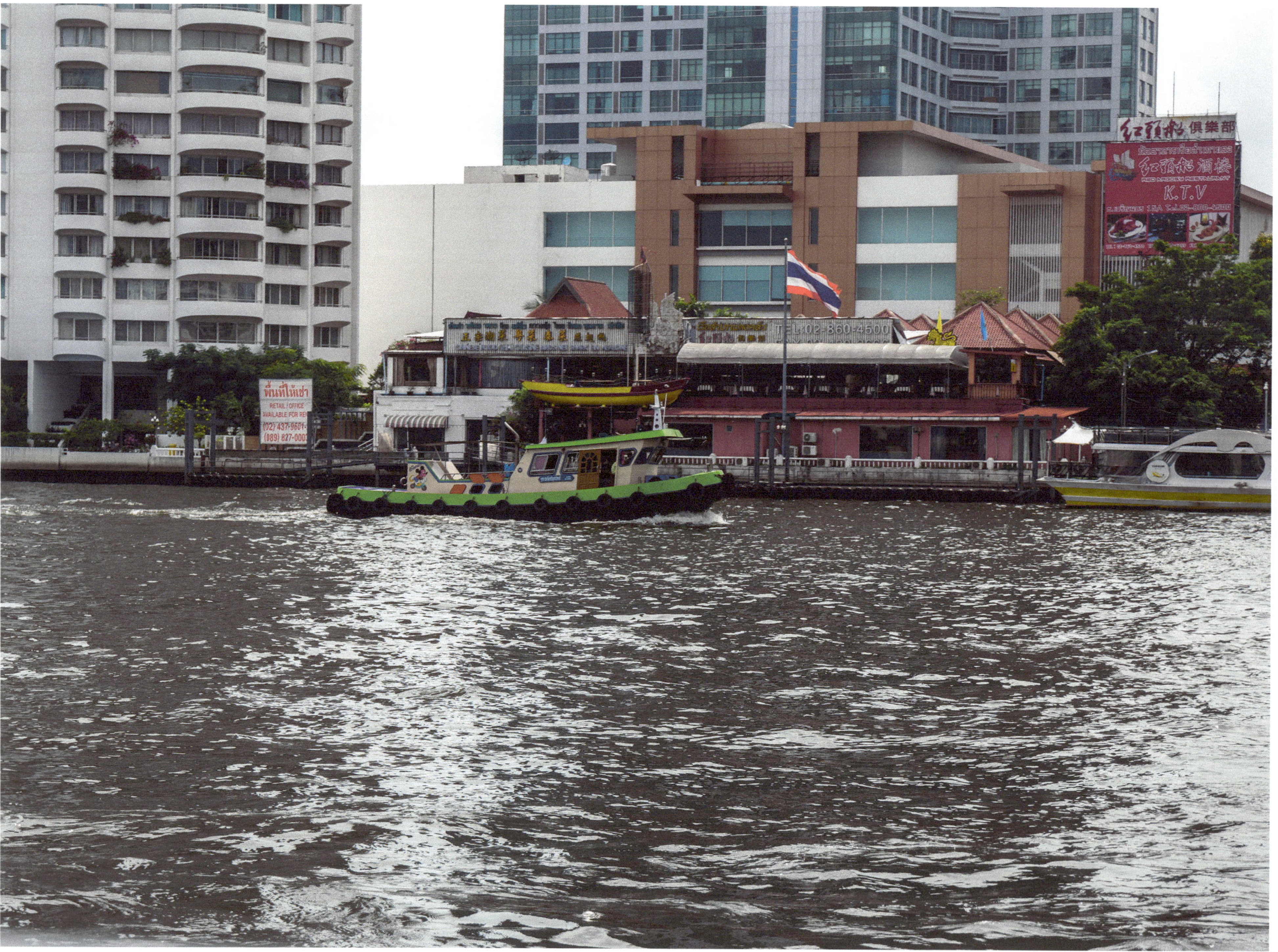
红頭船 俱樂部
红頭船 酒楼
K.T.V
พื้นที่ให้เช่า
RETAIL / OFFICE
TEL:02-860-4500

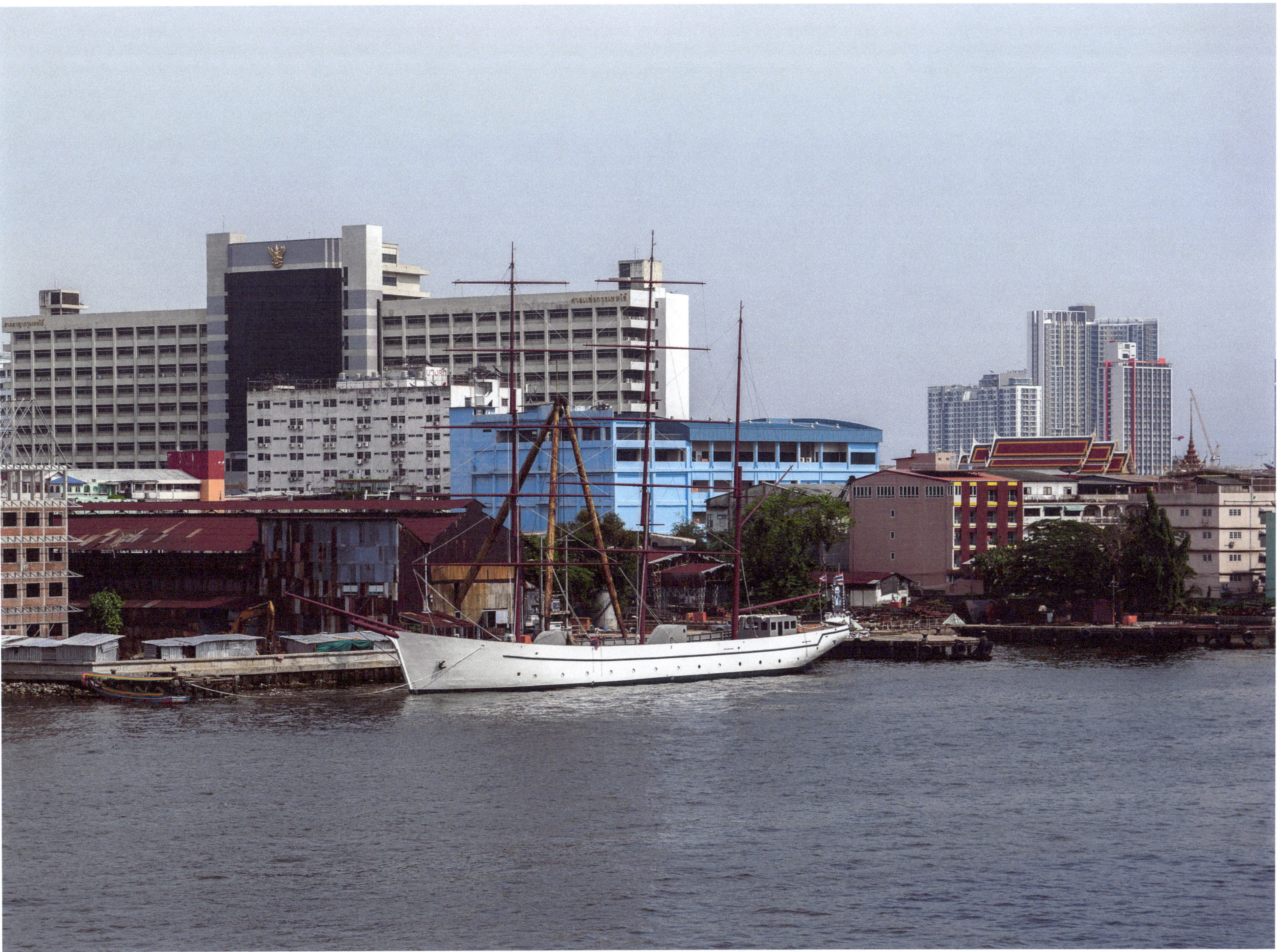

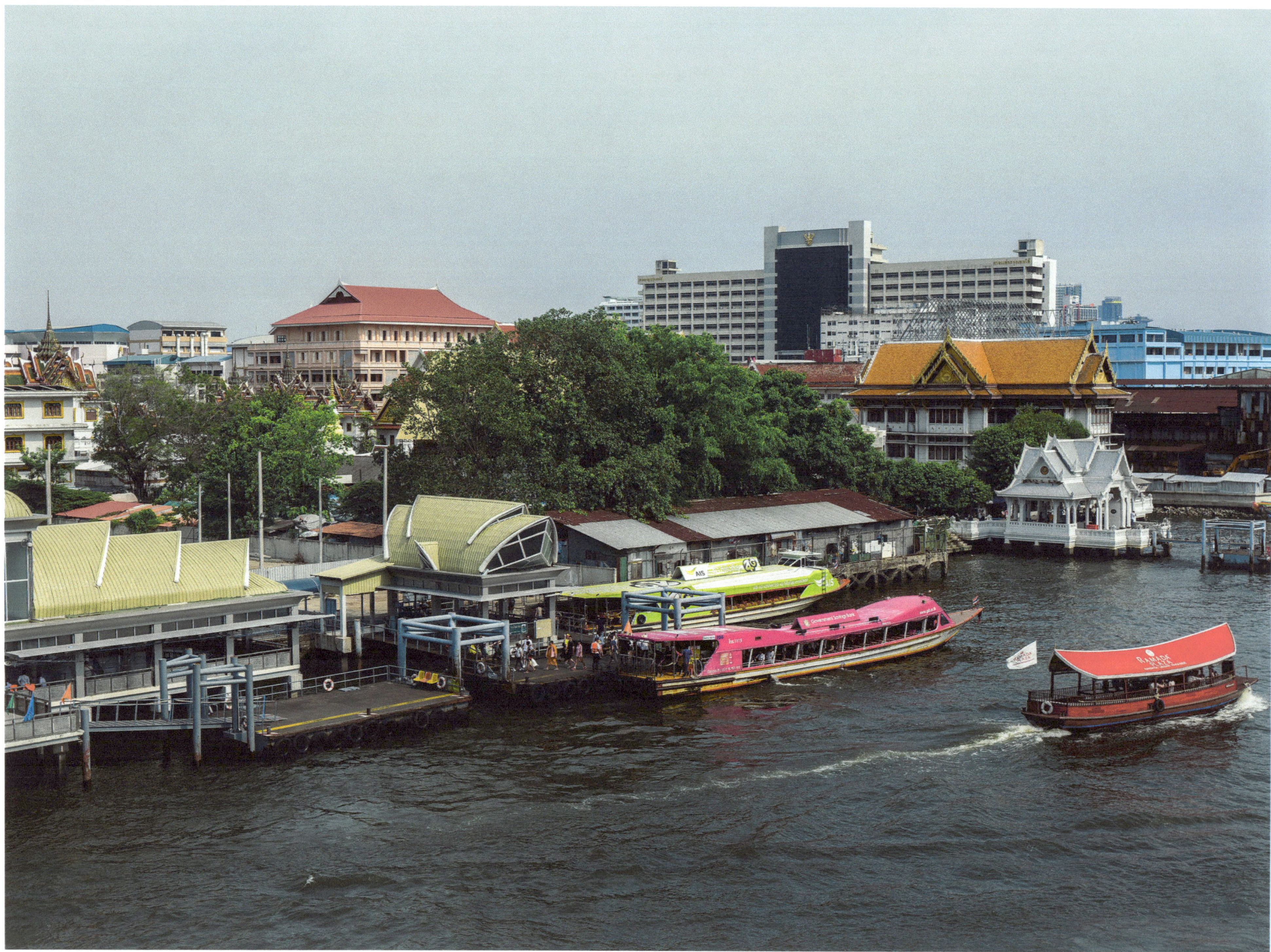
AIS

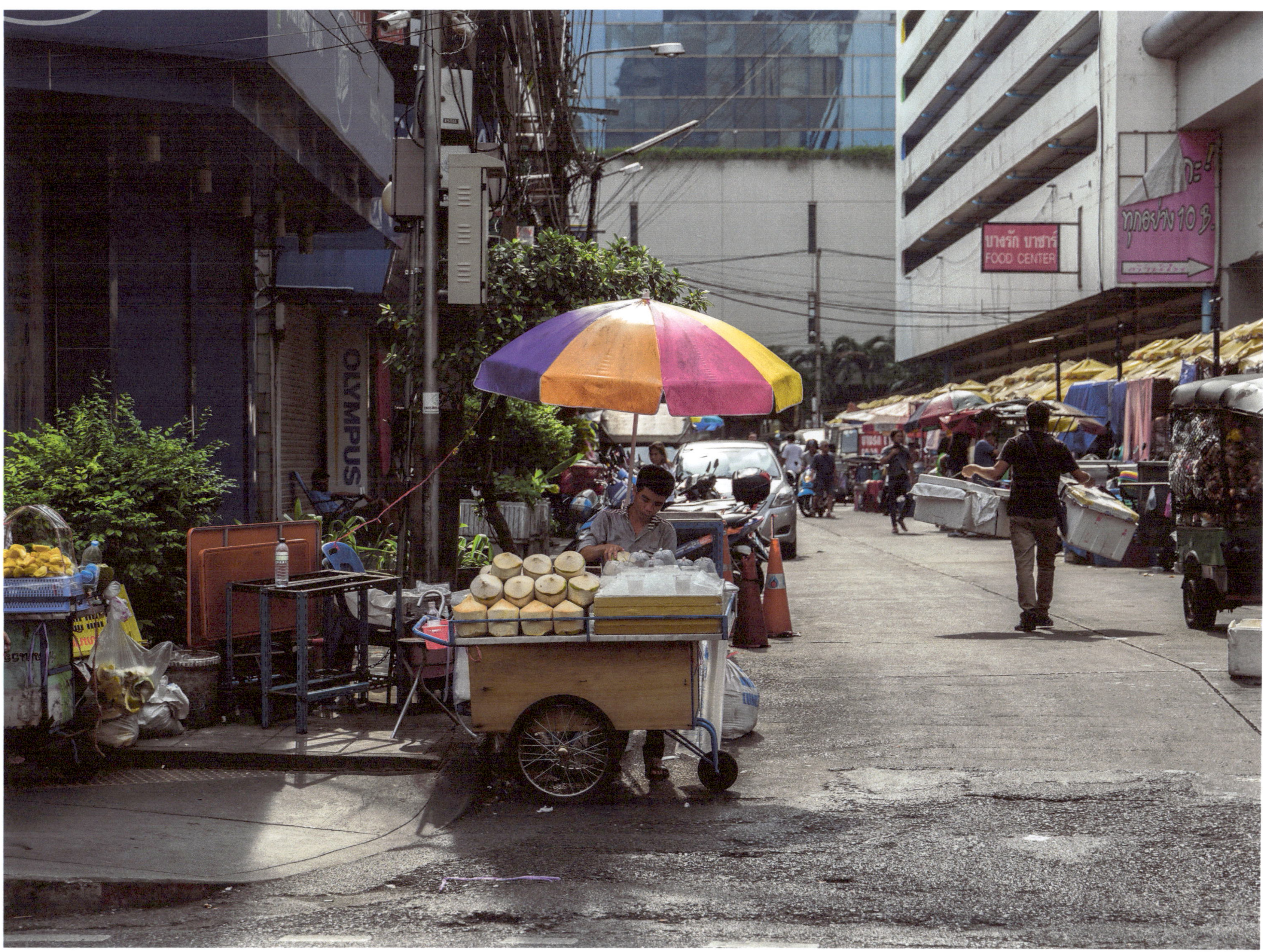
OLYMPUS
บางรัก บาซาร์
FOOD CENTER
ทุกอย่าง 10 ฿.

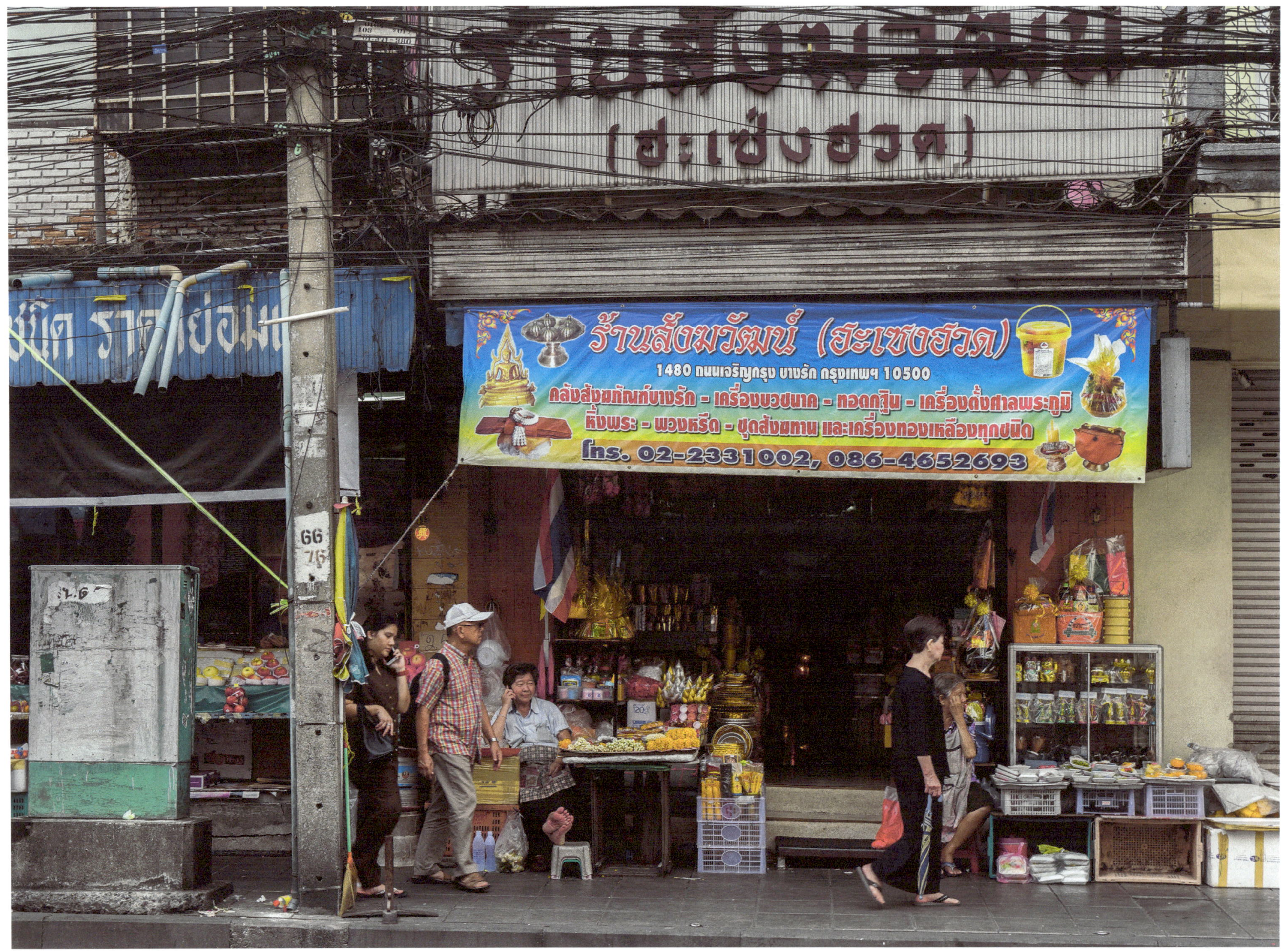
(ฮะเซ่งฮวด)
ร้านสังฆวัฒน์ (ฮะเซงฮวด)
1480 ถนนเจริญกรุง บางรัก กรุงเทพฯ 10500
คลังสังฆภัณฑ์บางรัก - เครื่องบวชนาค - ทอดกฐิน - เครื่องตั้งศาลพระภูมิ
หิ้งพระ - พวงหรีด - ชุดสังฆทาน และเครื่องทองเหลืองทุกชนิด
โทร. 02-2331002, 086-4652693
66

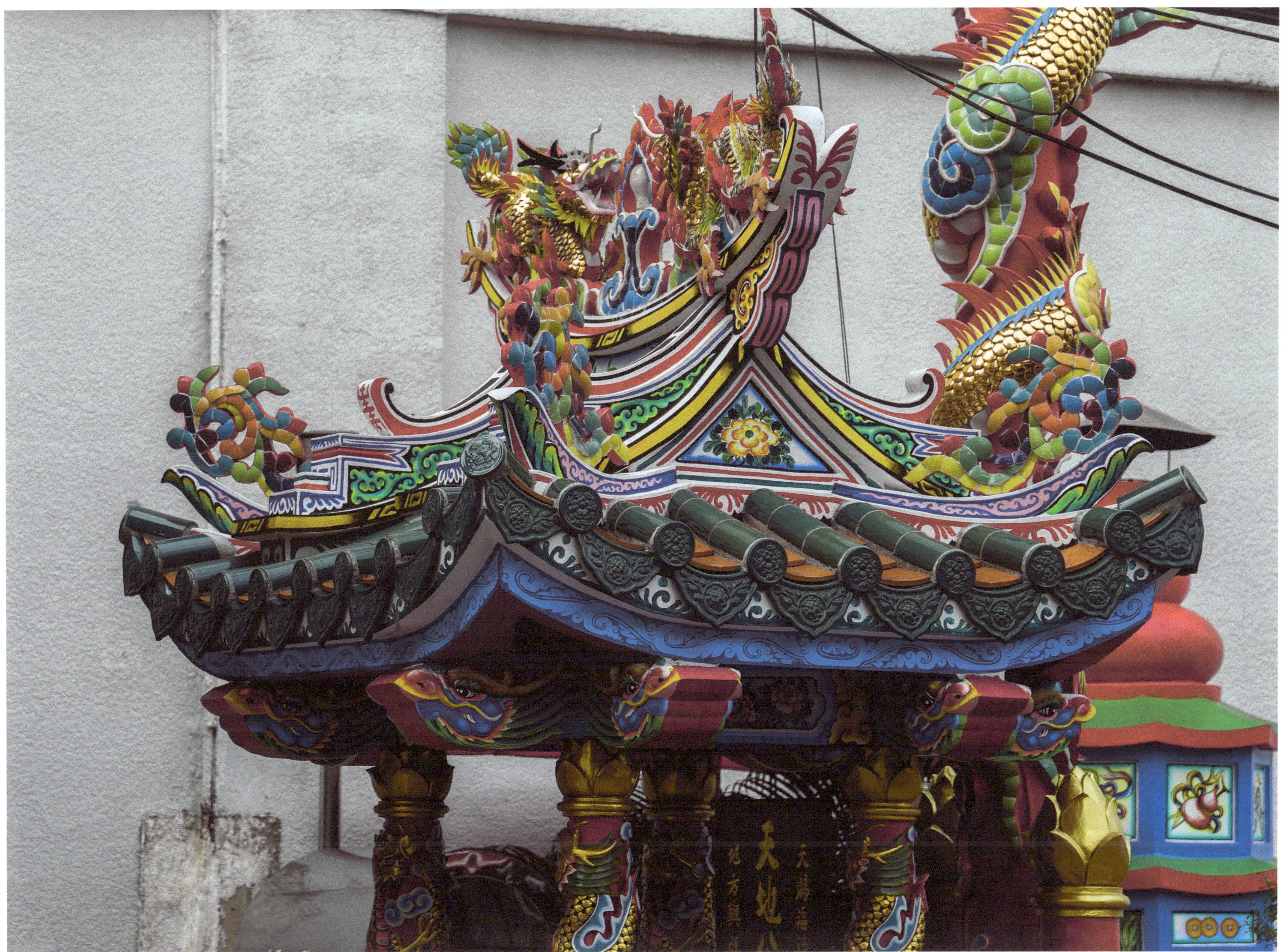
天地

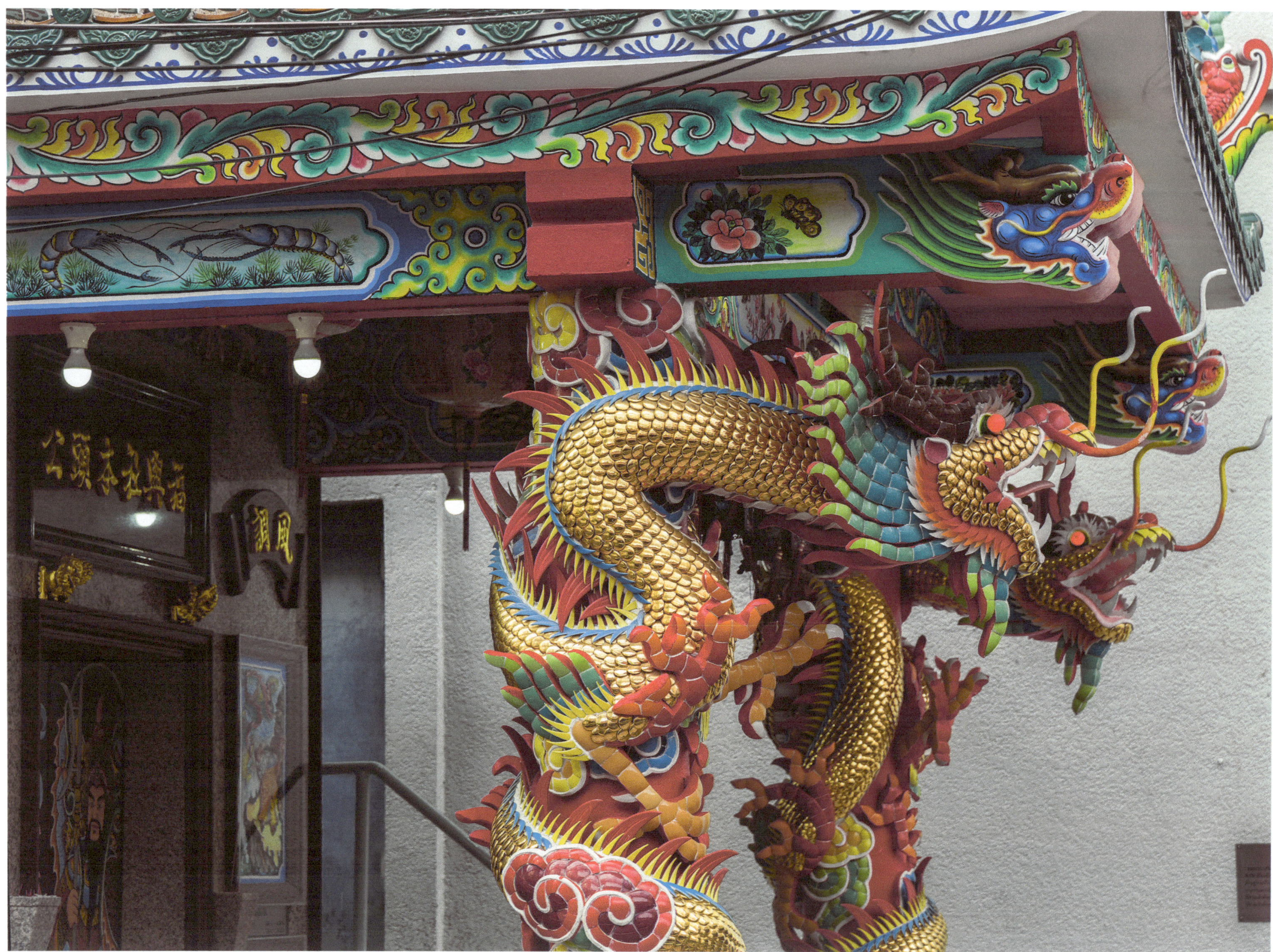

福興社本頭公
風調

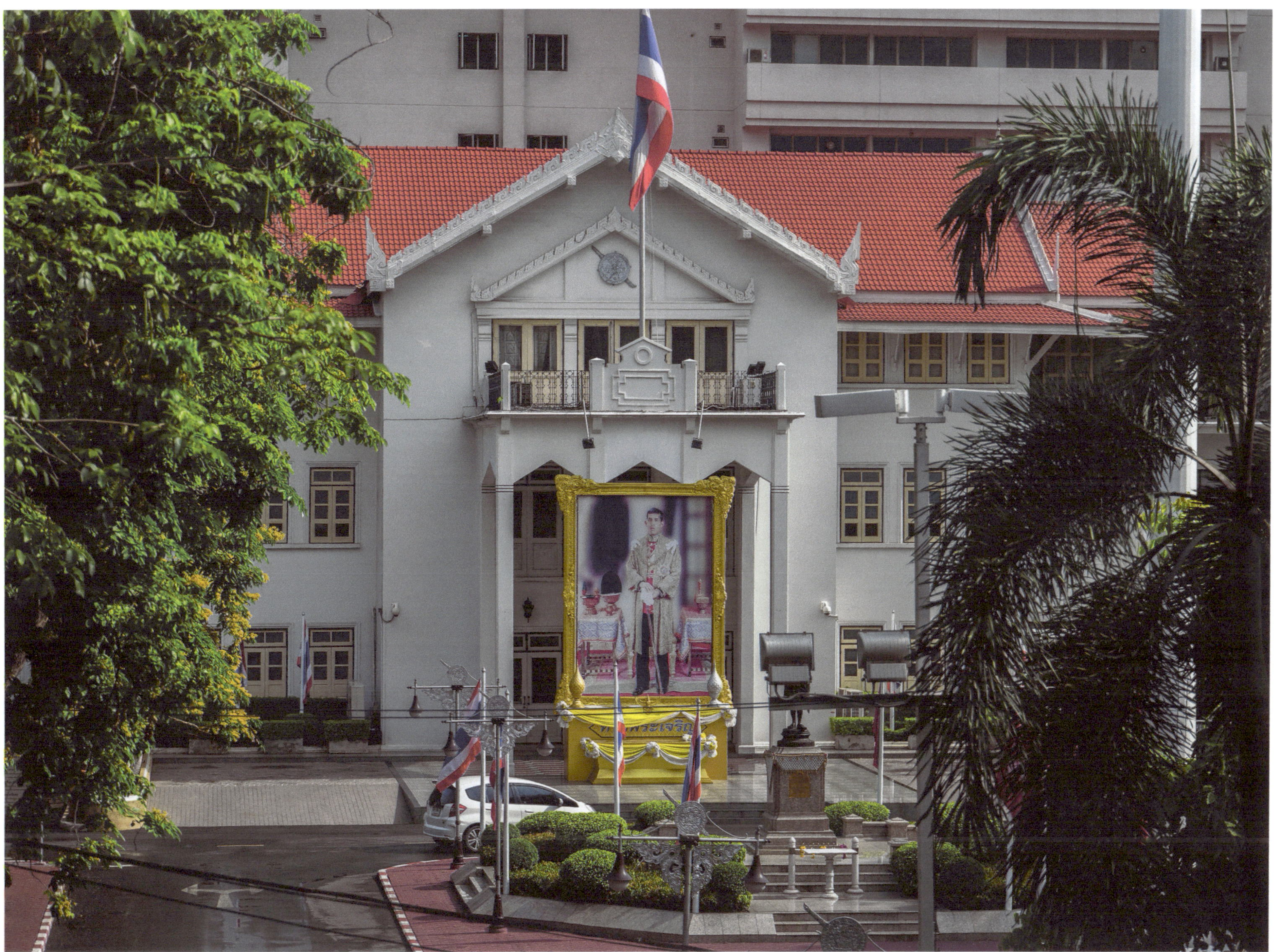

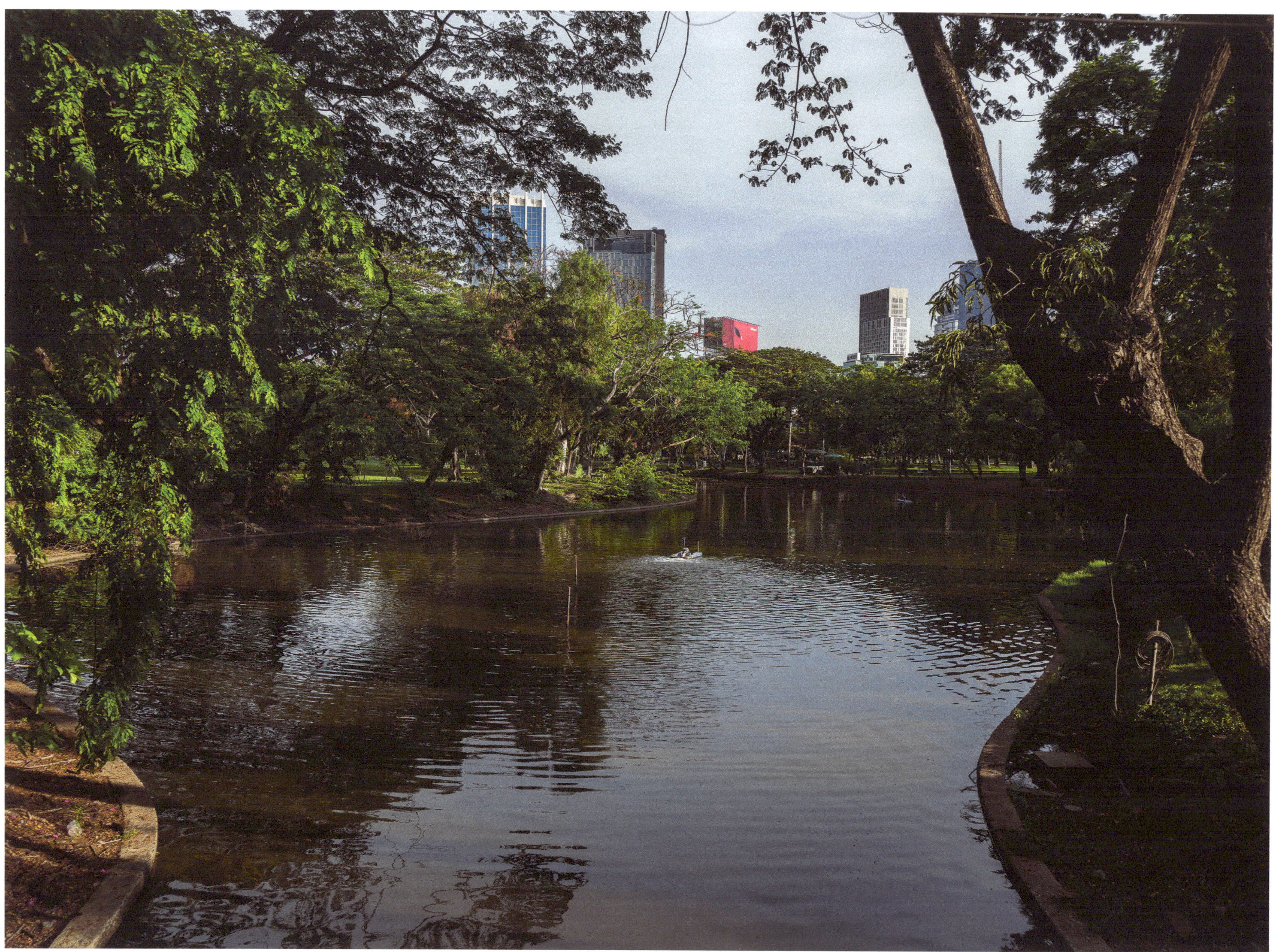

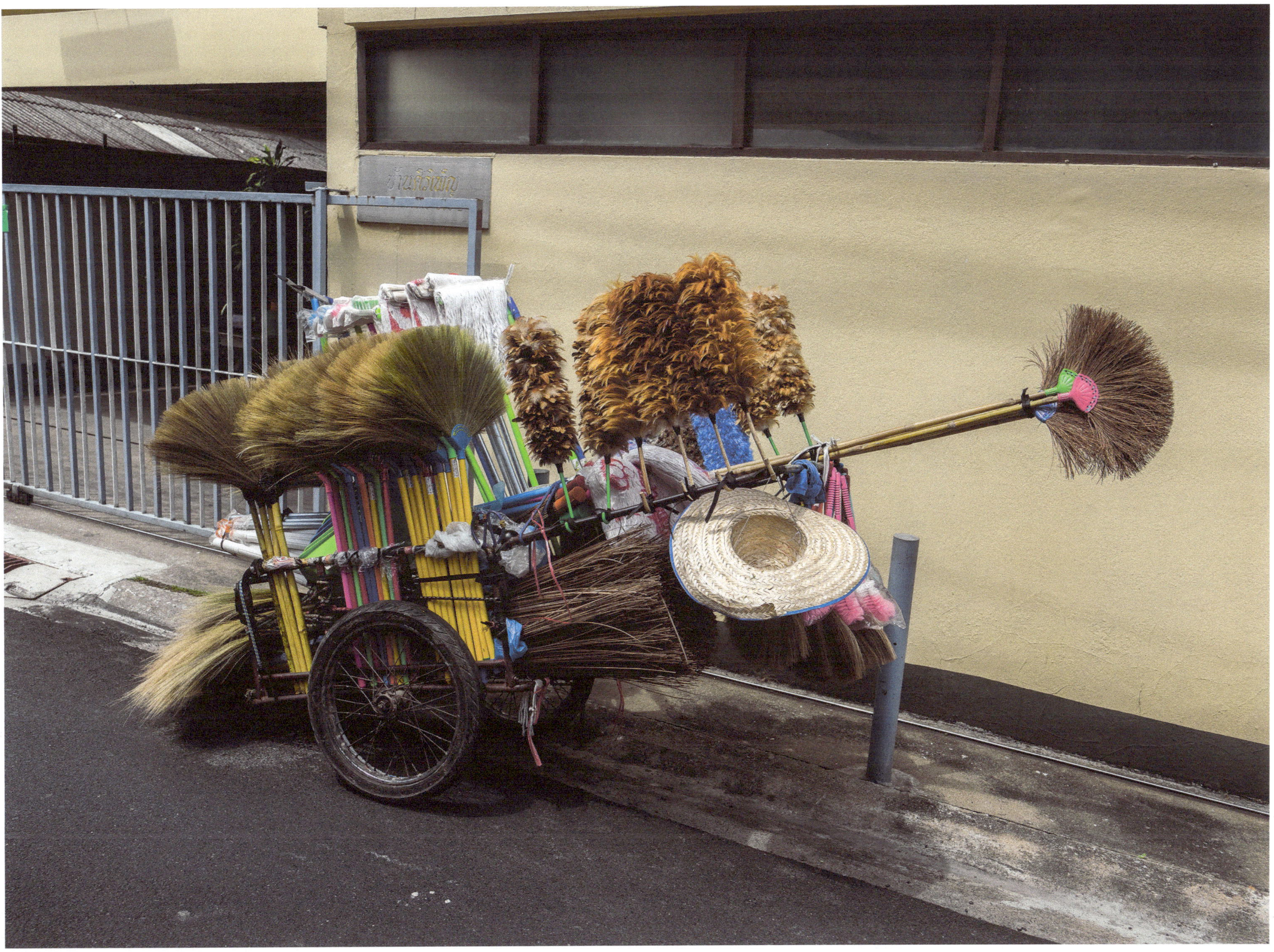

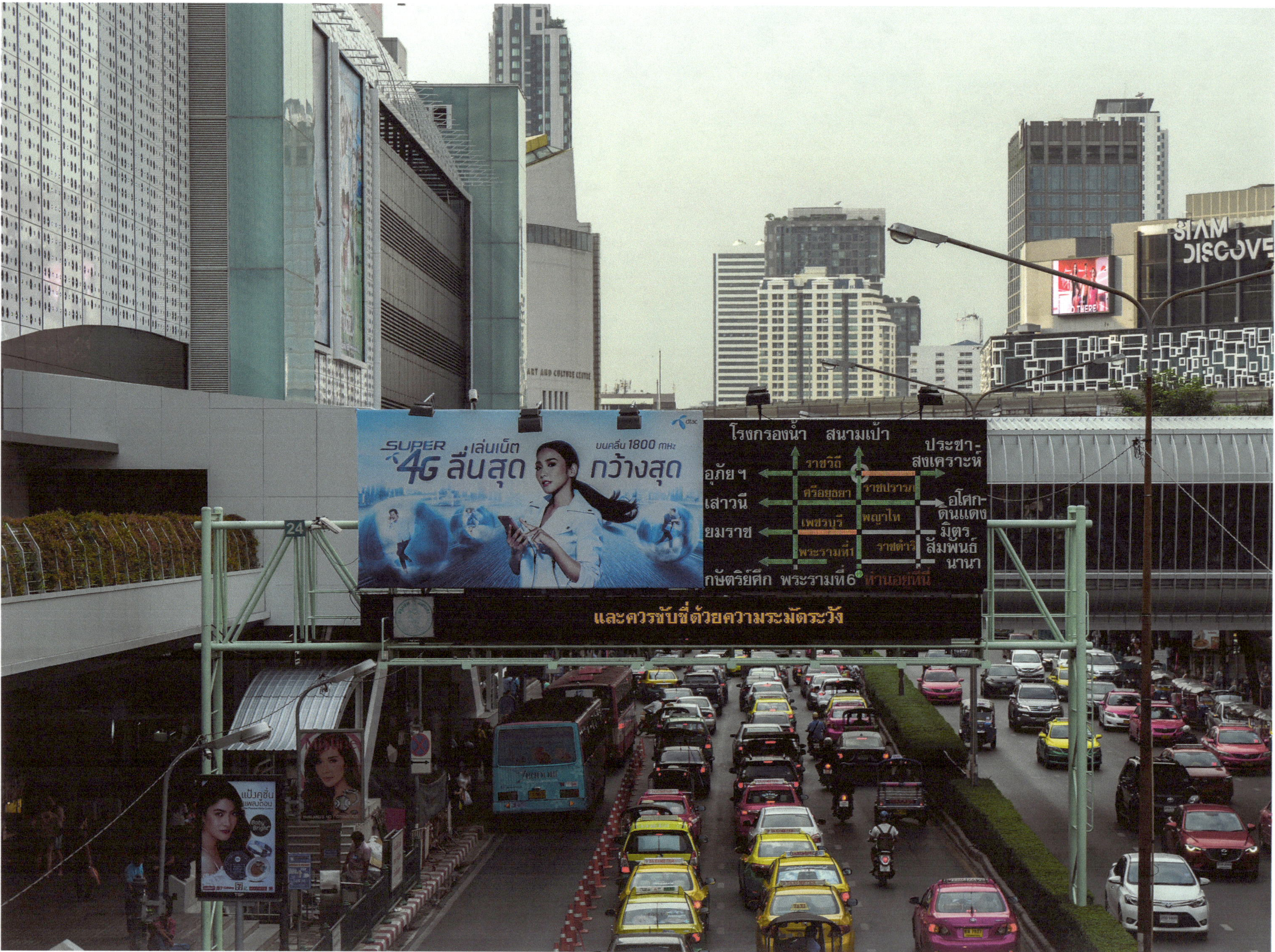

SUPER 4G
เล่นเน็ต ลื่นสุด กว้างสุด
บนคลื่น 1800 MHz
โรงกรองน้ำ
สนามเป้า
ประชา-สงเคราะห์
อุภัย ฯ
เสาวนี
อโศก-ดินแดง
ยมราช
มิตร สัมพันธ์
นานา
กษัตริย์ศึก
พระรามที่6
และควรขับขี่ด้วยความระมัดระวัง

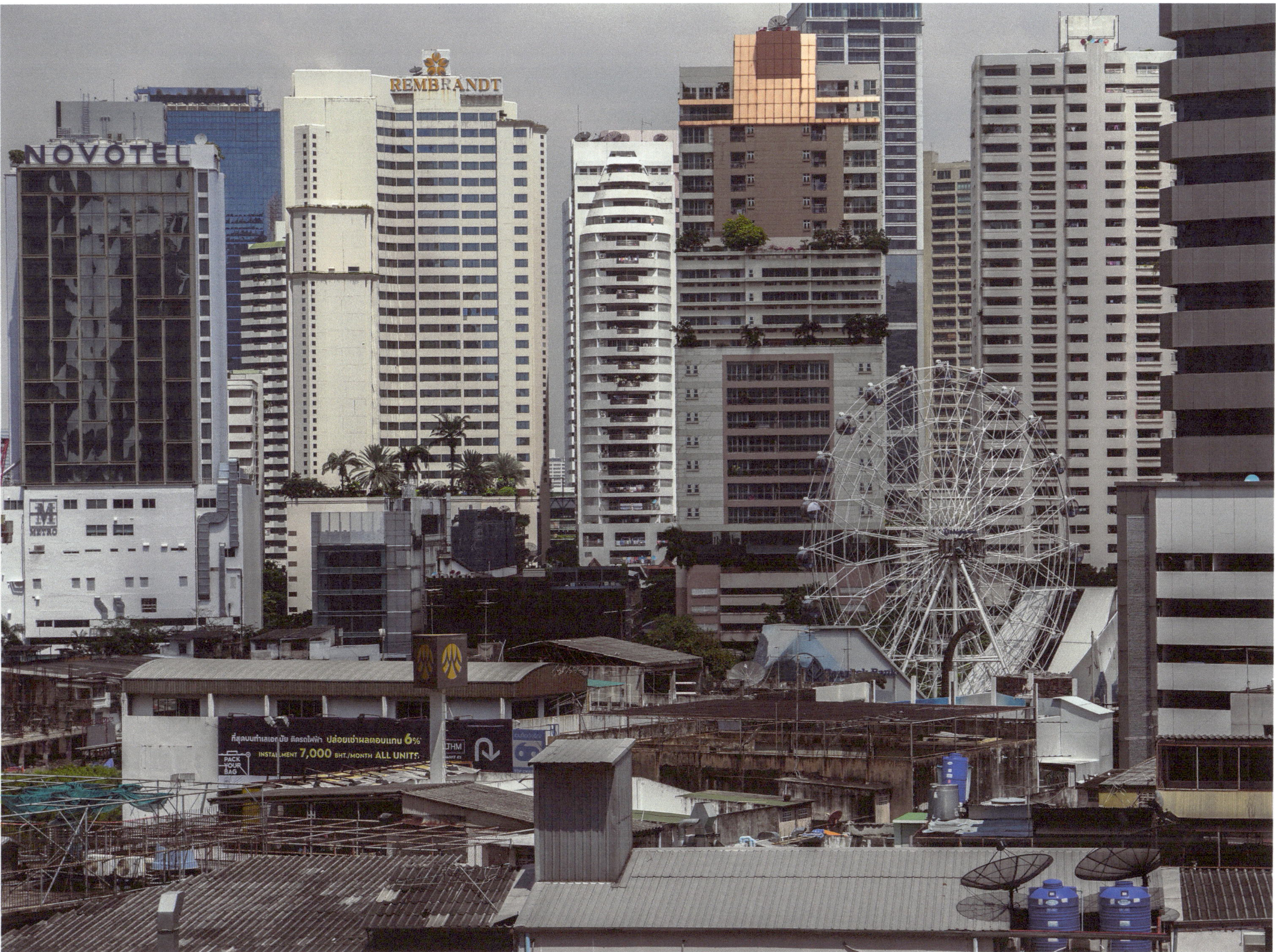
NOVOTEL
REMBRANDT
METRO
ปล่อยเช่าผลตอบแทน 6%
INSTALLMENT 7,000 BHT./MONTH ALL UNITS
PACK YOUR BAG

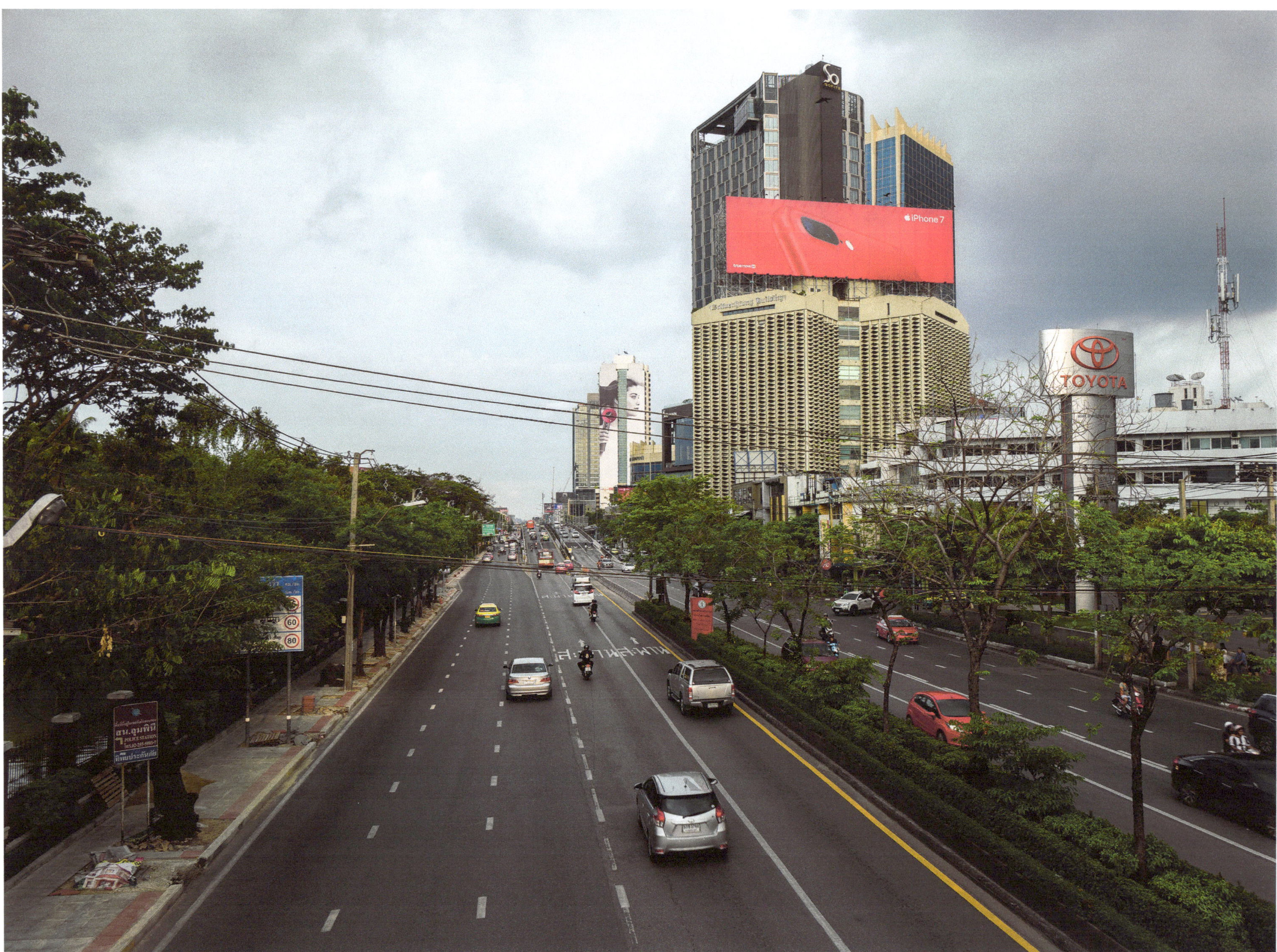
iPhone 7
TOYOTA
60
80

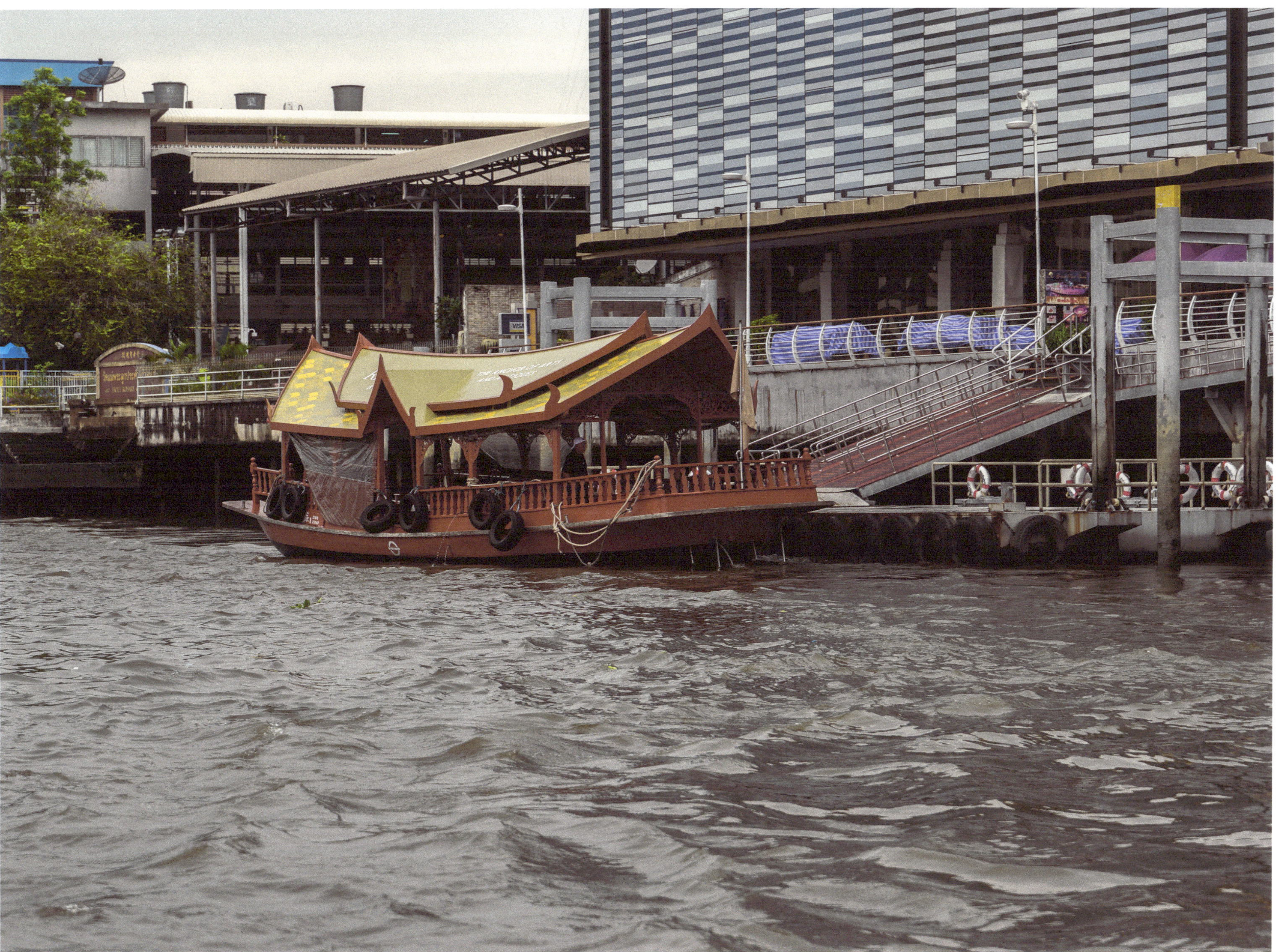

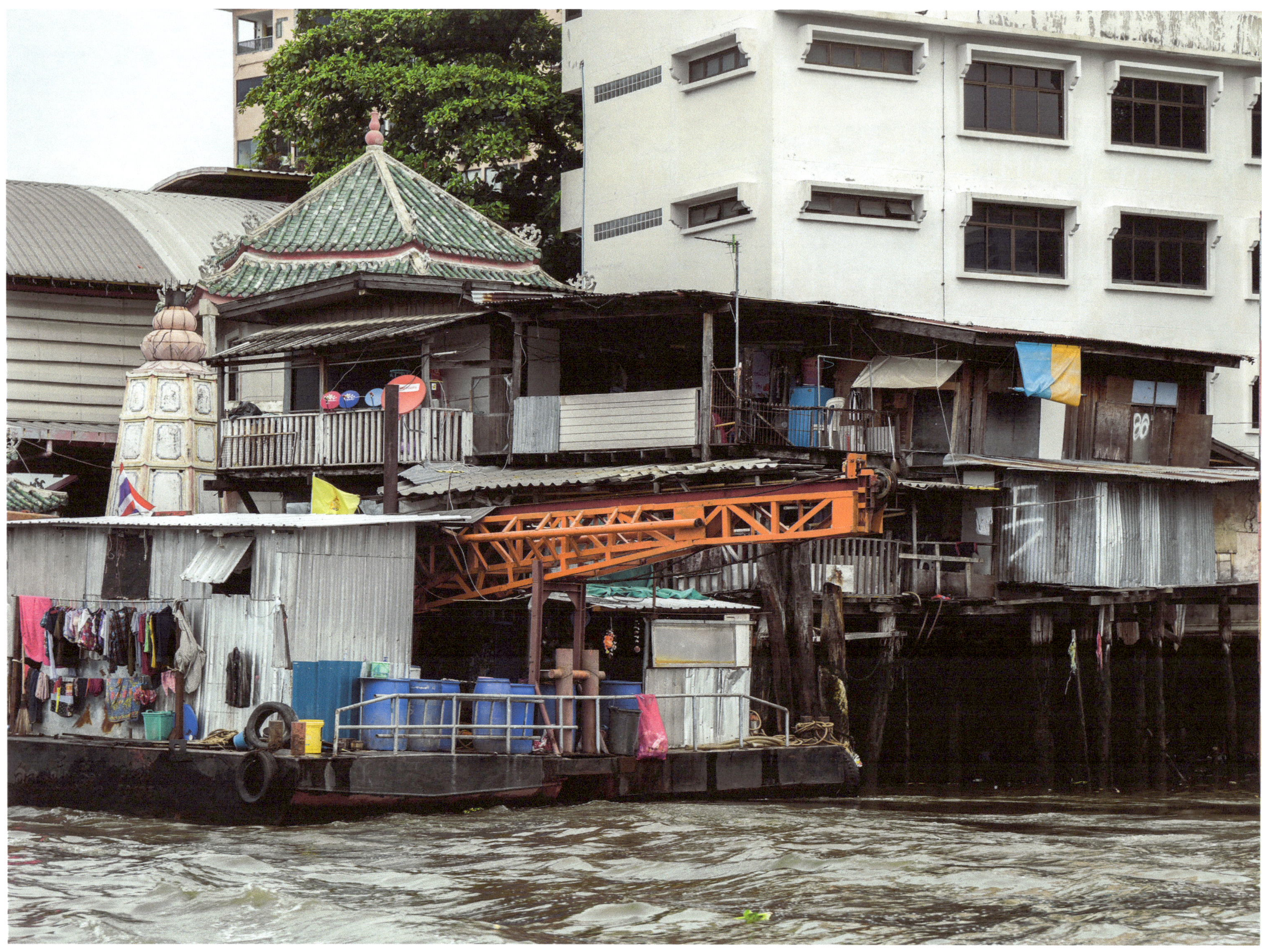

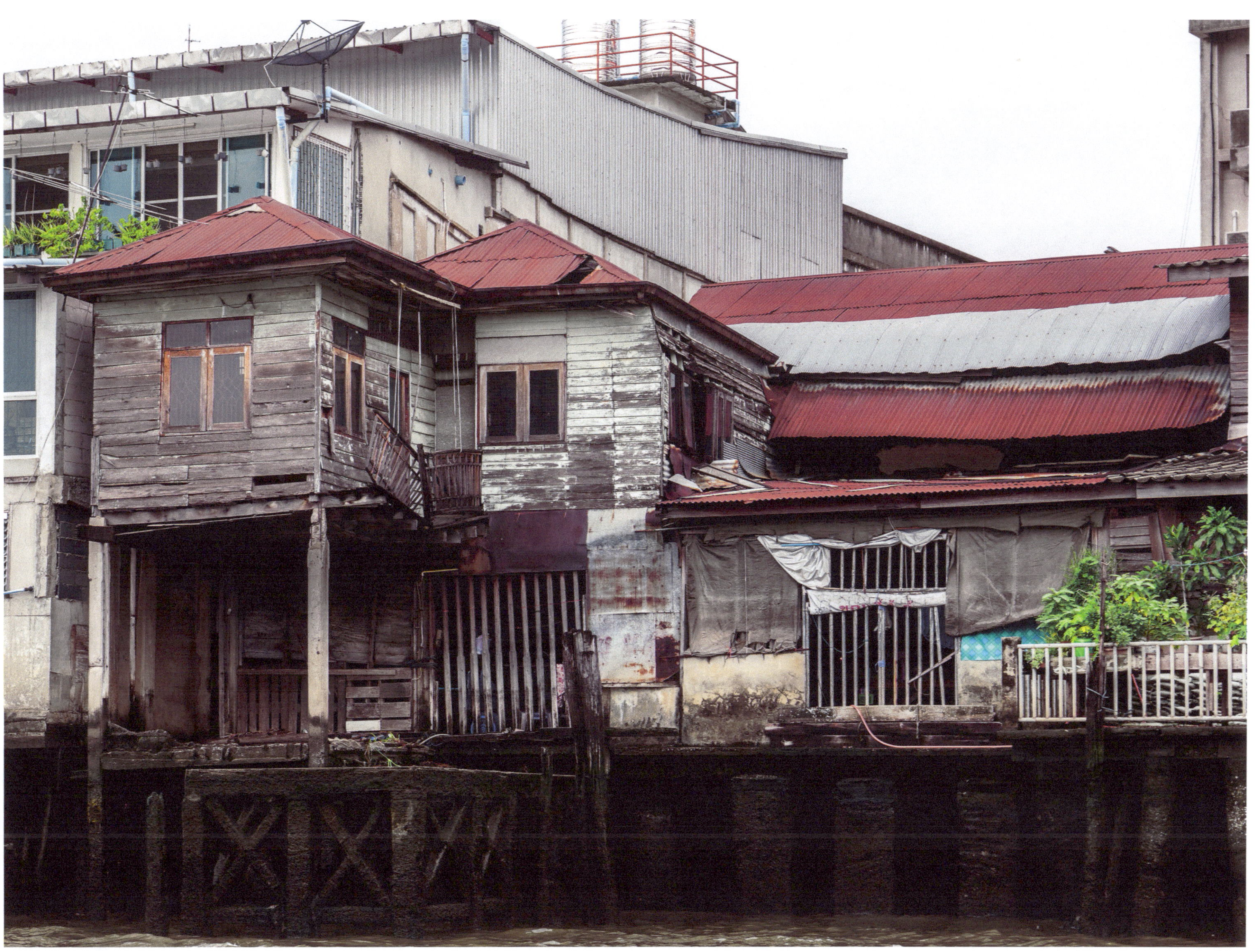

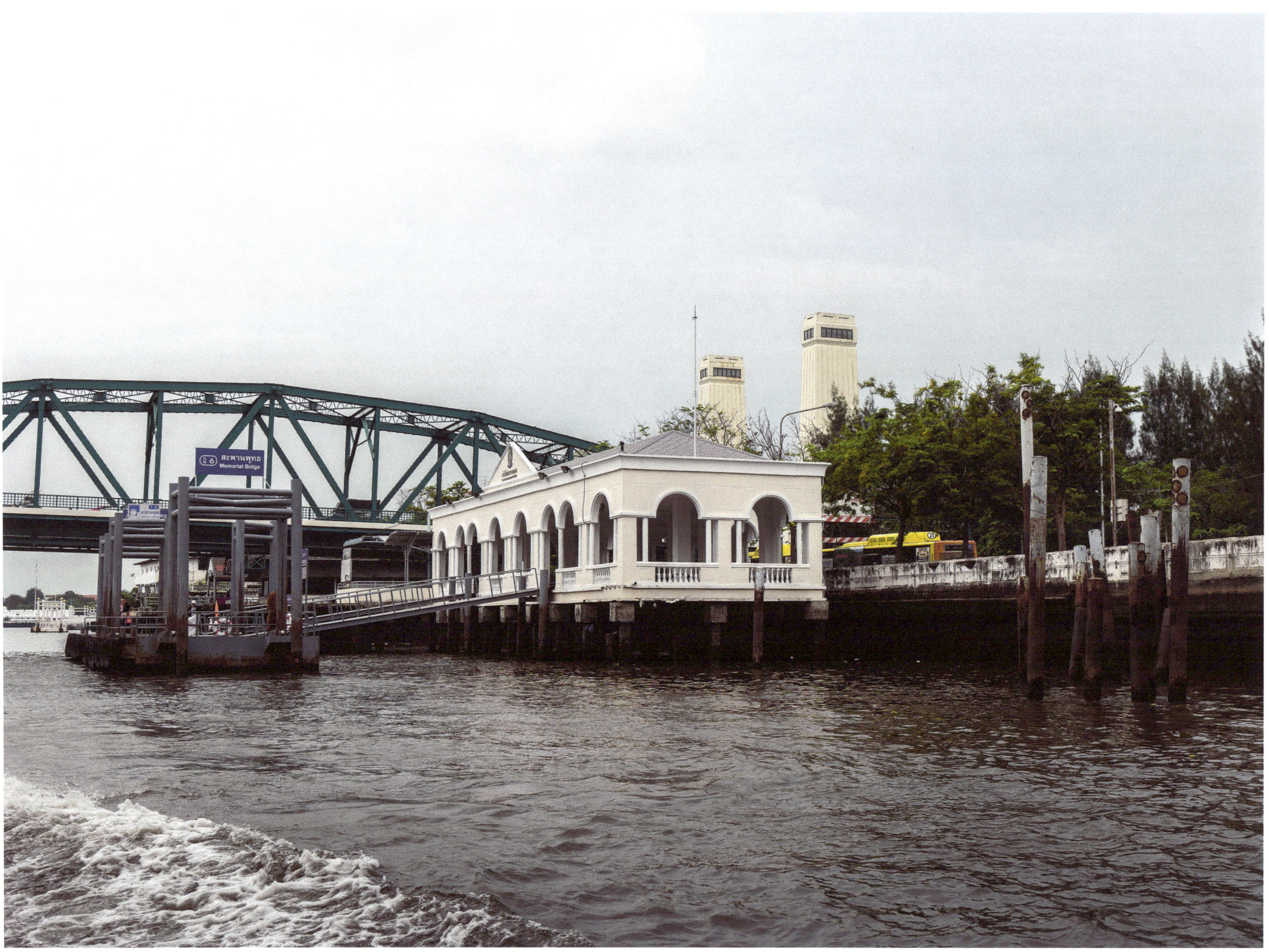
น N 6
สะพานพุทธ
Memorial Bidge

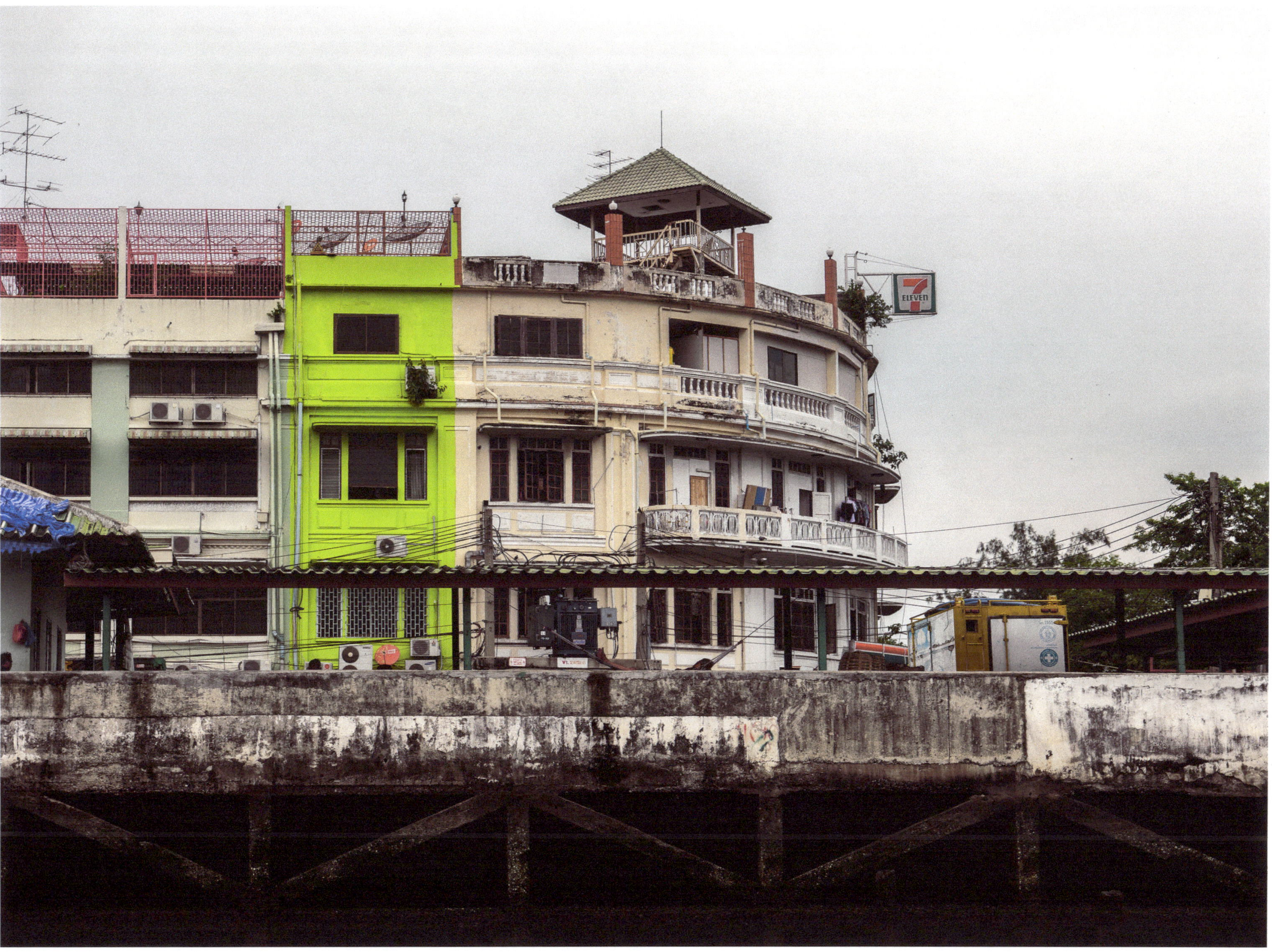
7
ELEVEn

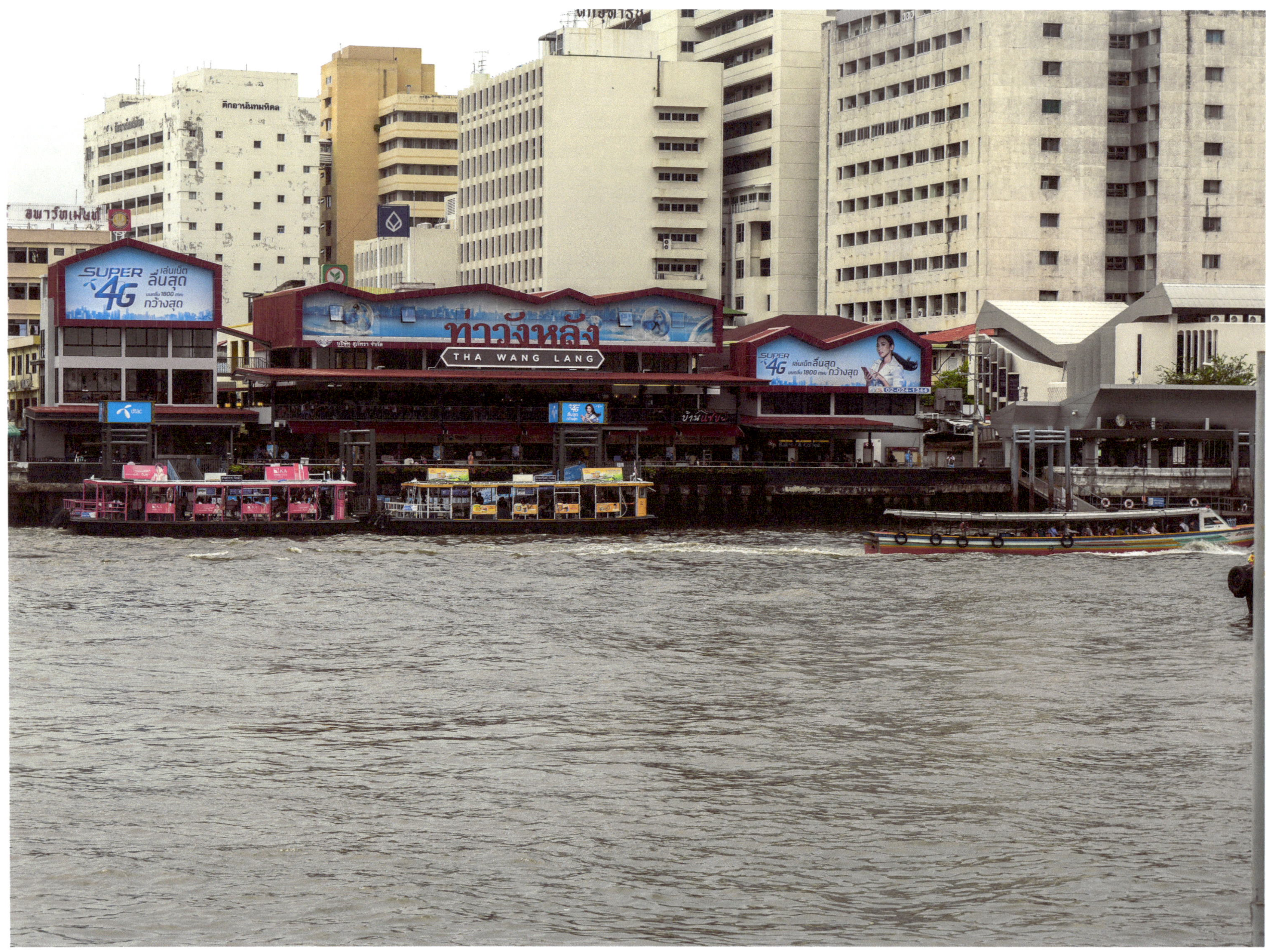
SUPER 4G
เล่นเน็ต ลื่นสุด
กว้างสุด
ท่าวังหลัง
THA WANG LANG
SUPER 4G
เล่นเน็ต ลื่นสุด
กว้างสุด
02-024-1344
dtac

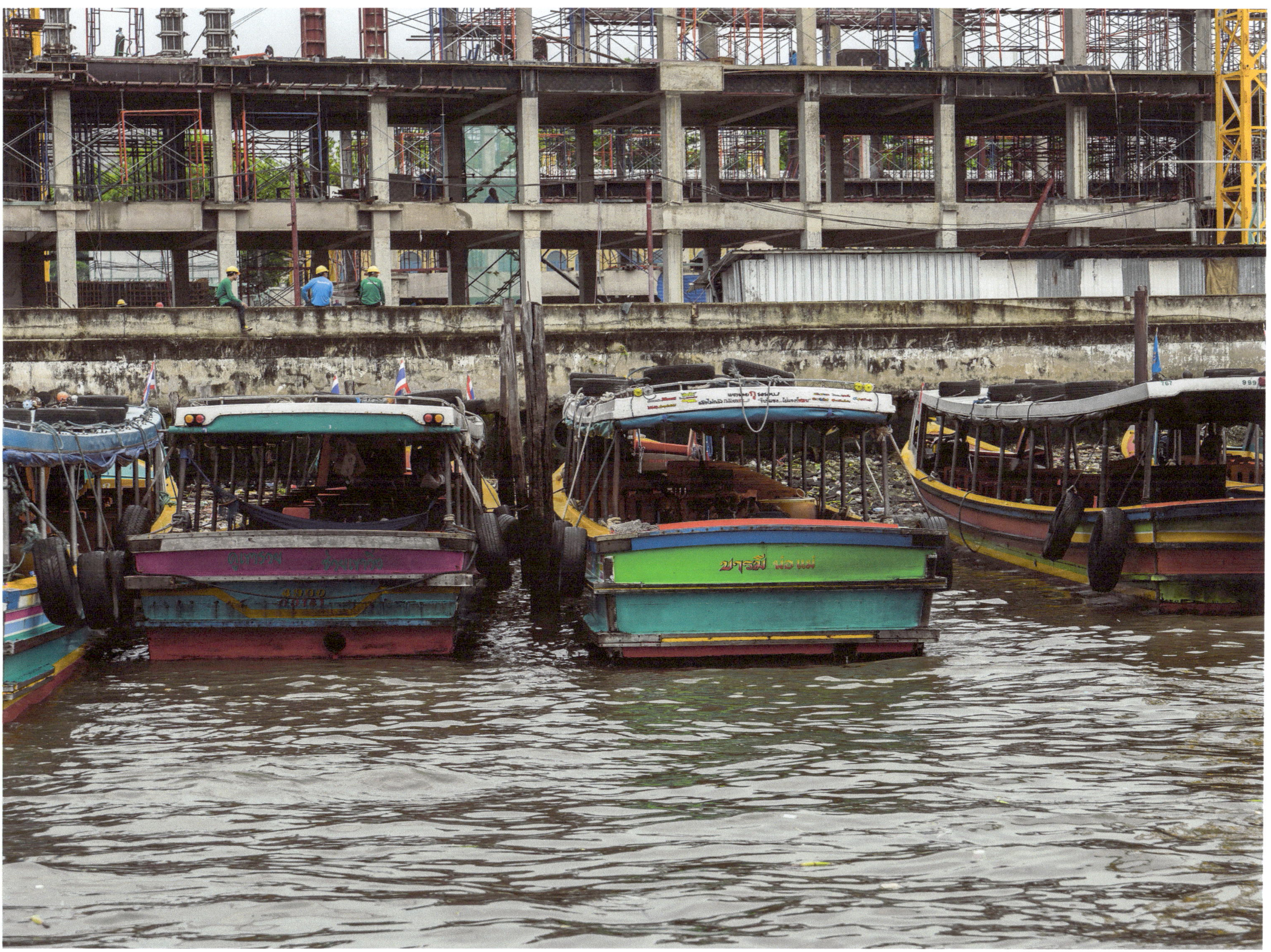

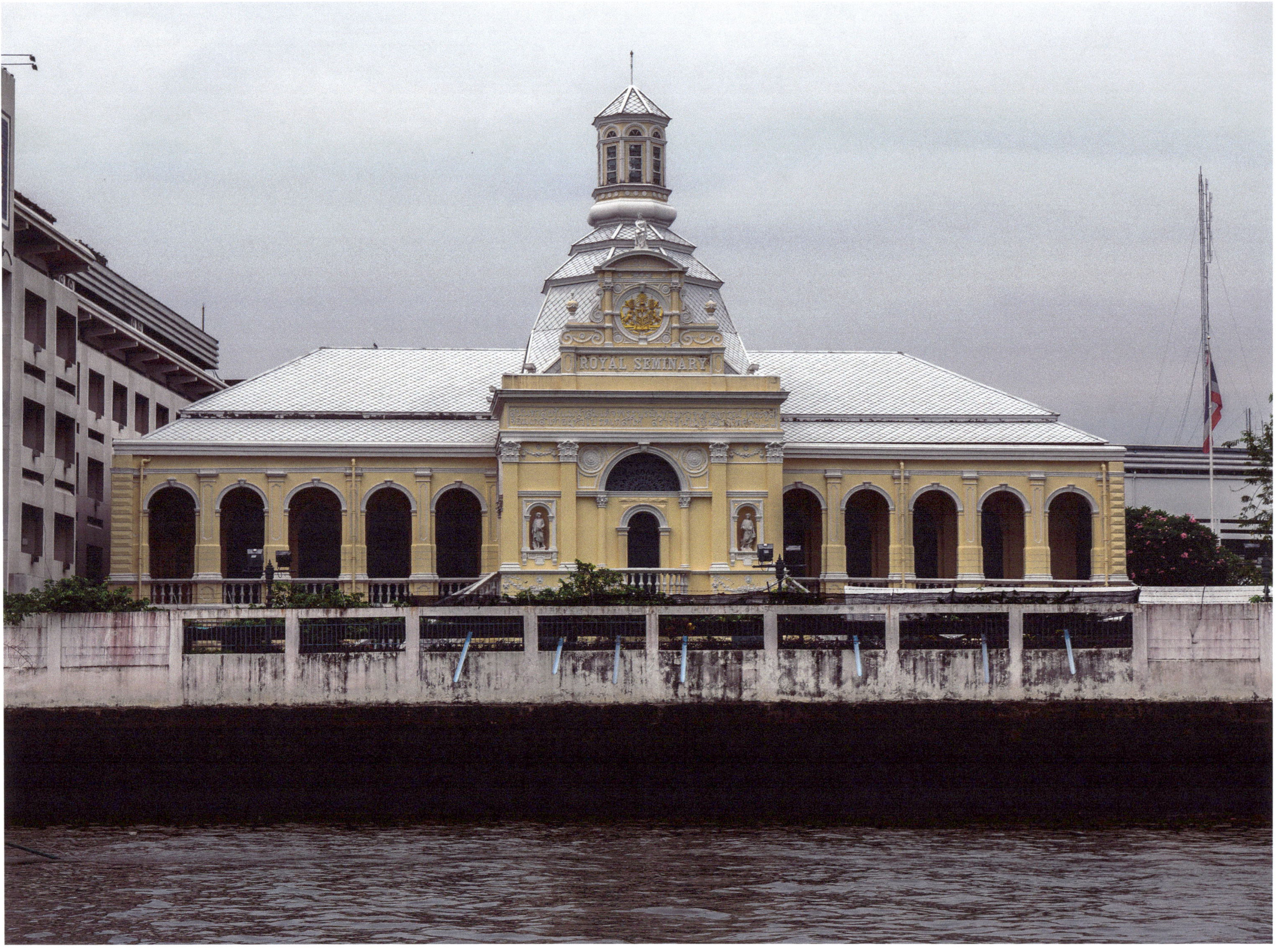
ROYAL SEMINARY

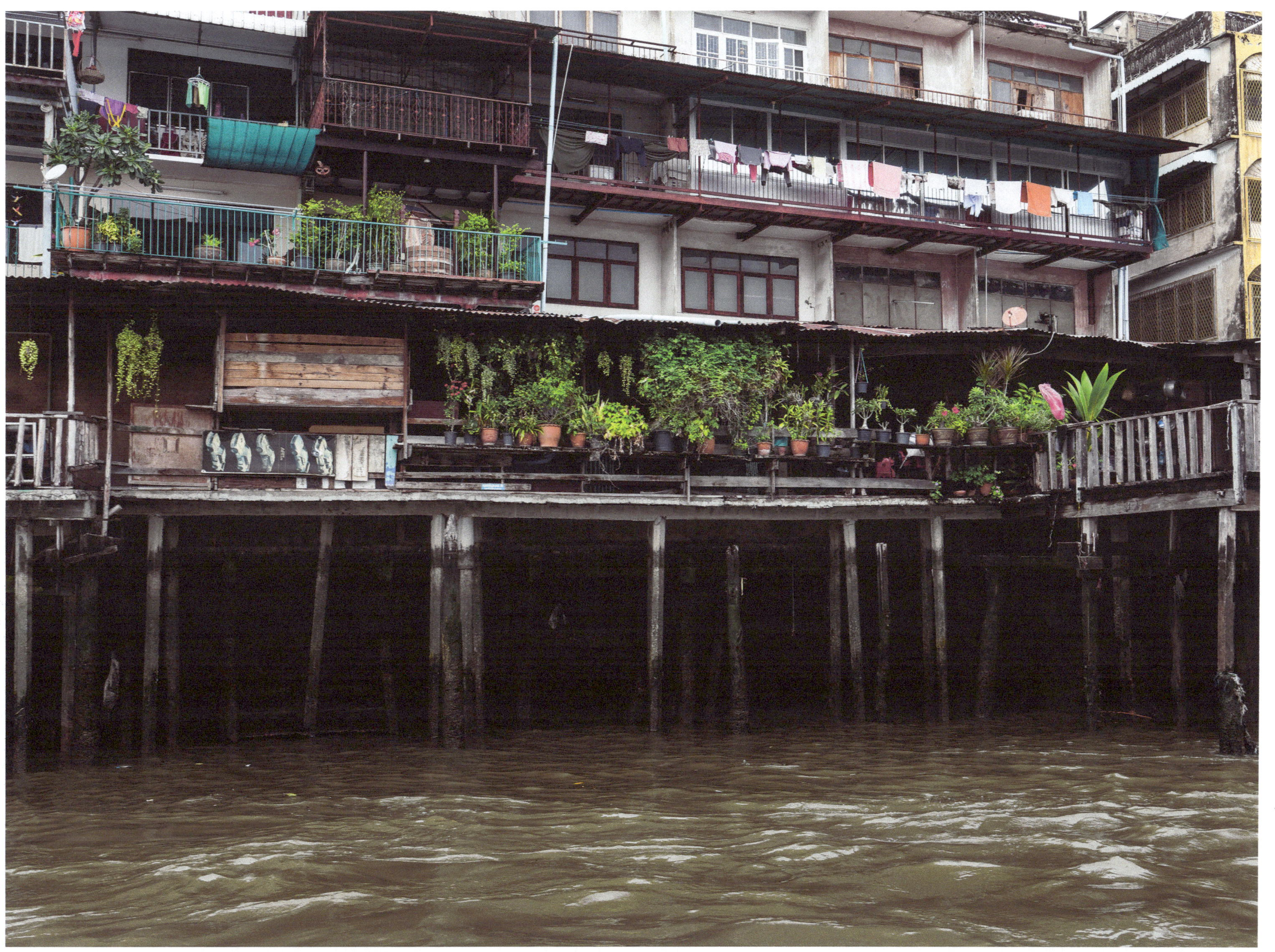

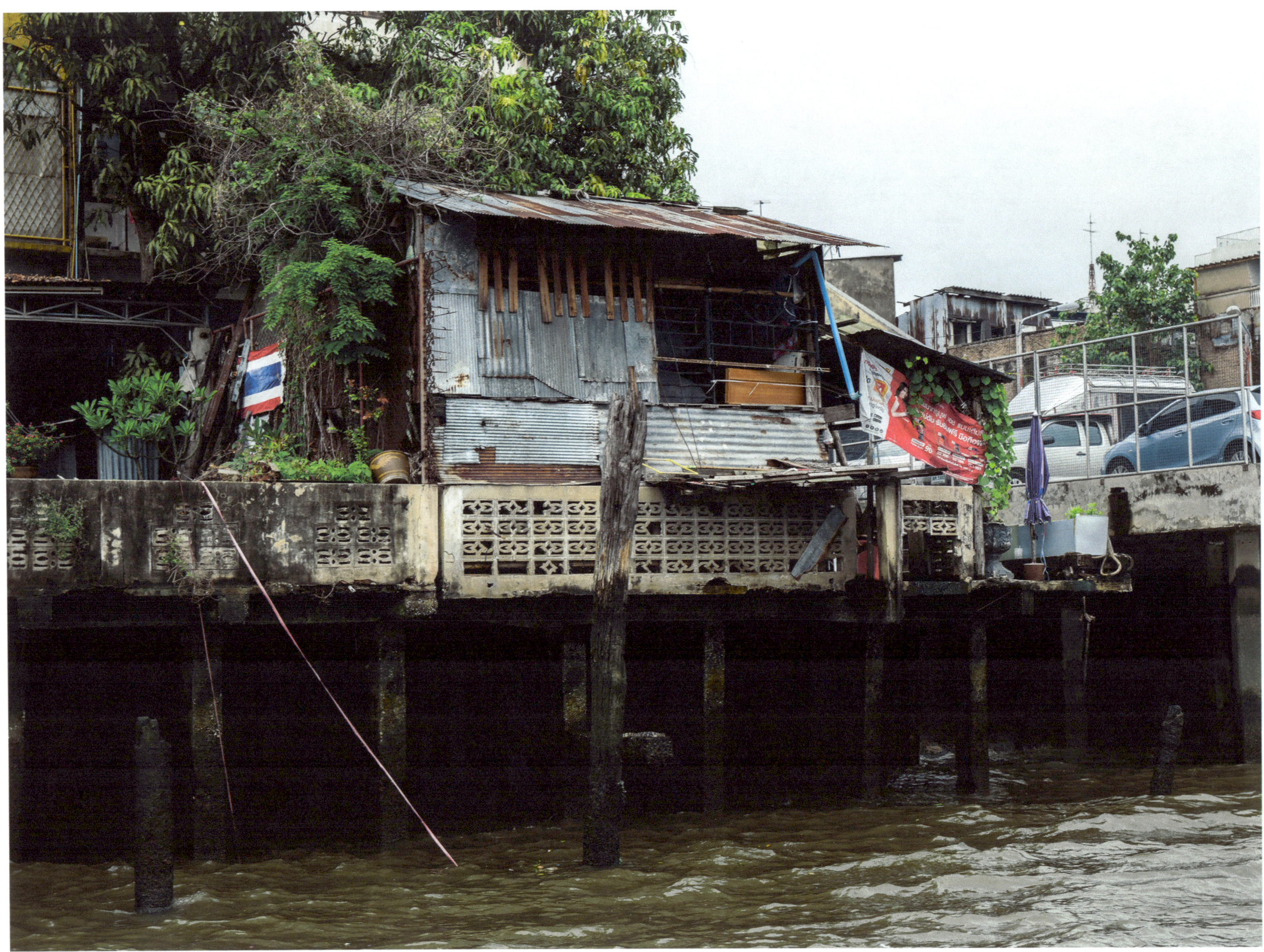

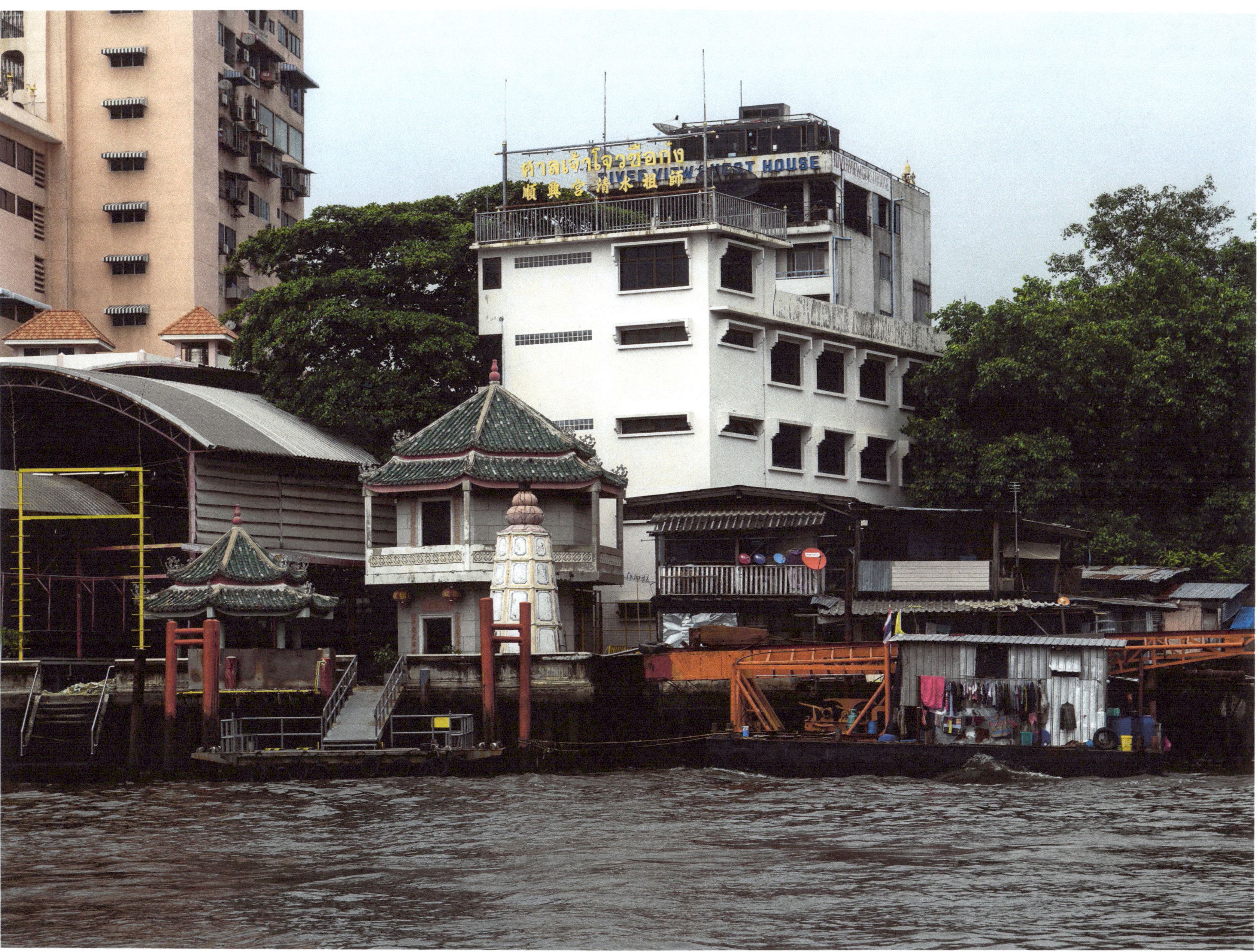
ศาลเจ้าโจวซือกง
順興宮清水祖師
HOUSE

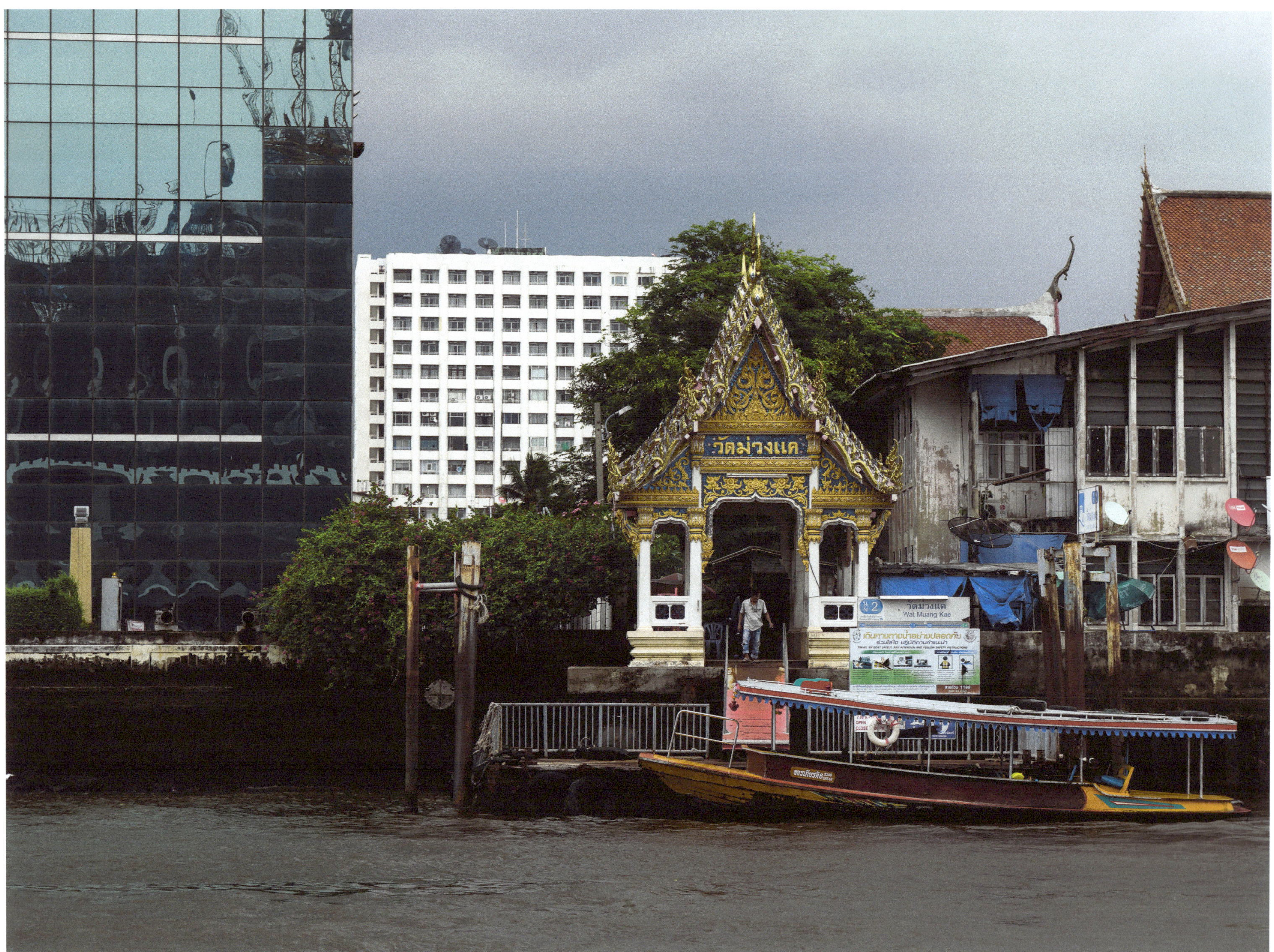
วัดม่วงแค
2
วัดม่วงแค
Wat Muang Kae
เดินทางทางน้ำอย่างปลอดภัย
ร่วมใส่ใจ ปฏิบัติตามคำแนะนำ
TRAVEL BY BOAT SAFELY, PAY ATTENTION AND FOLLOW SAFETY INSTRUCTIONS
สายด่วน 1199
OPEN
CLOSE

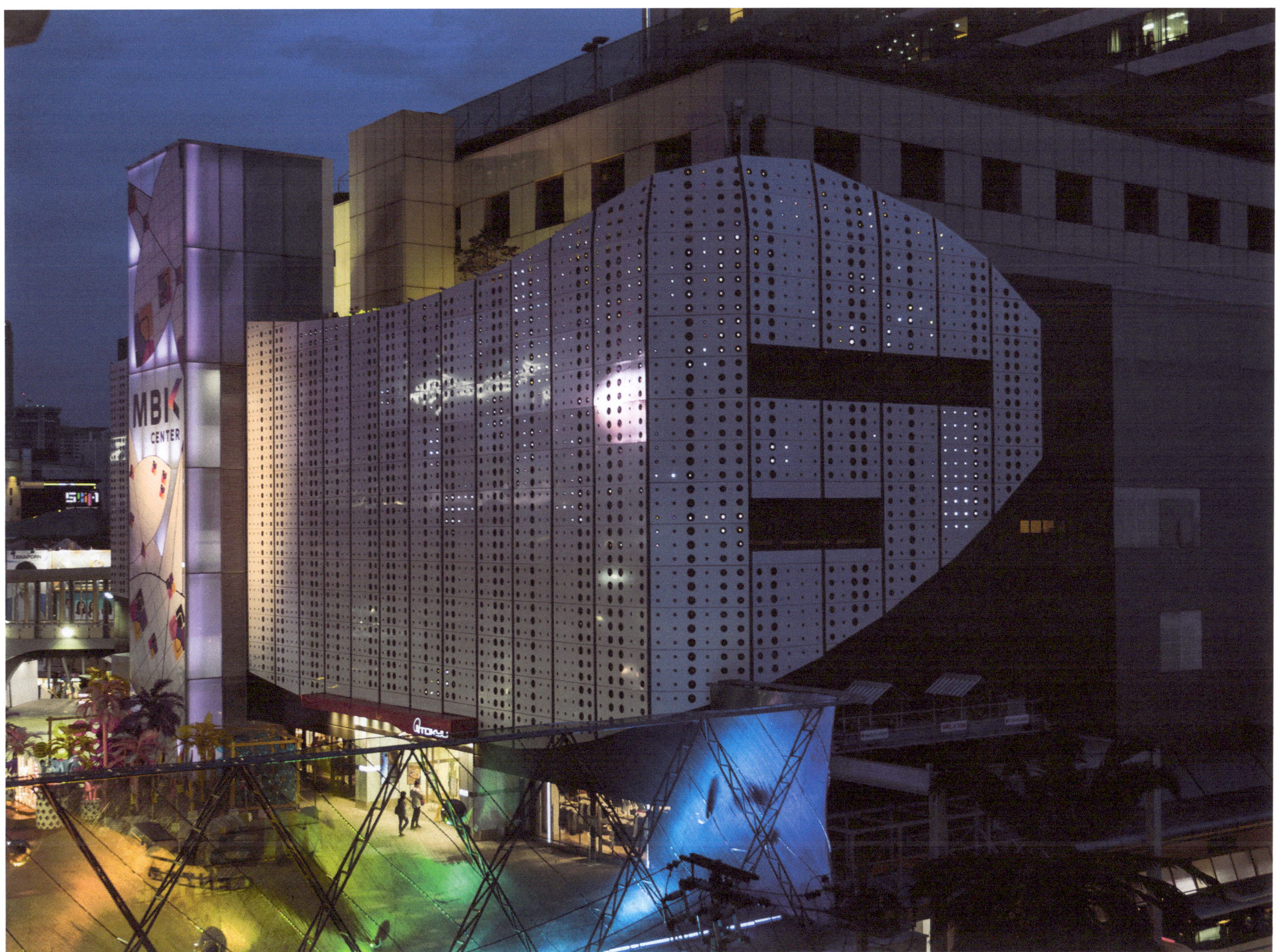
MBK
CENTER

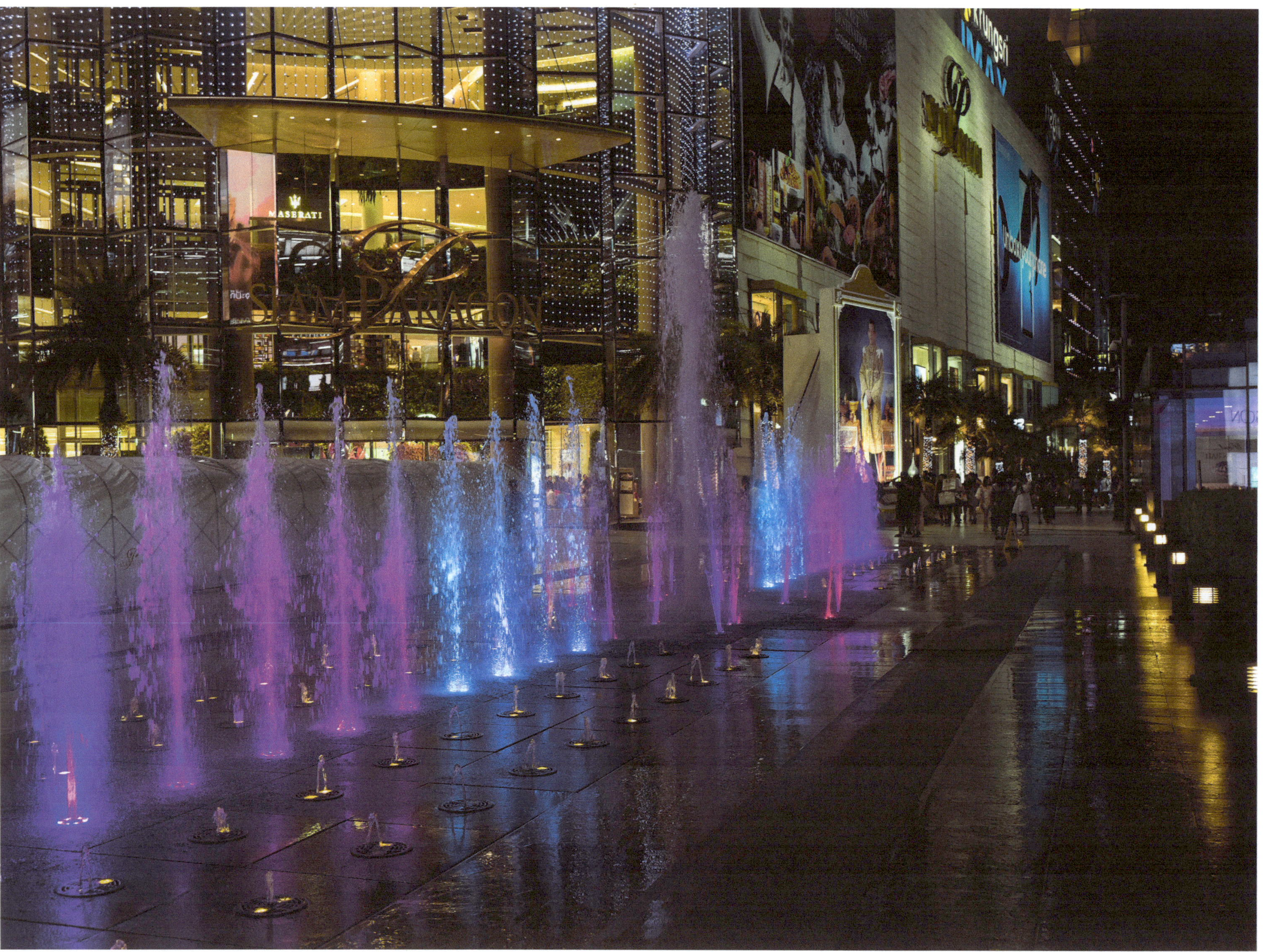
MASERATI
SIAM PARAGON
krungsri
IMAX

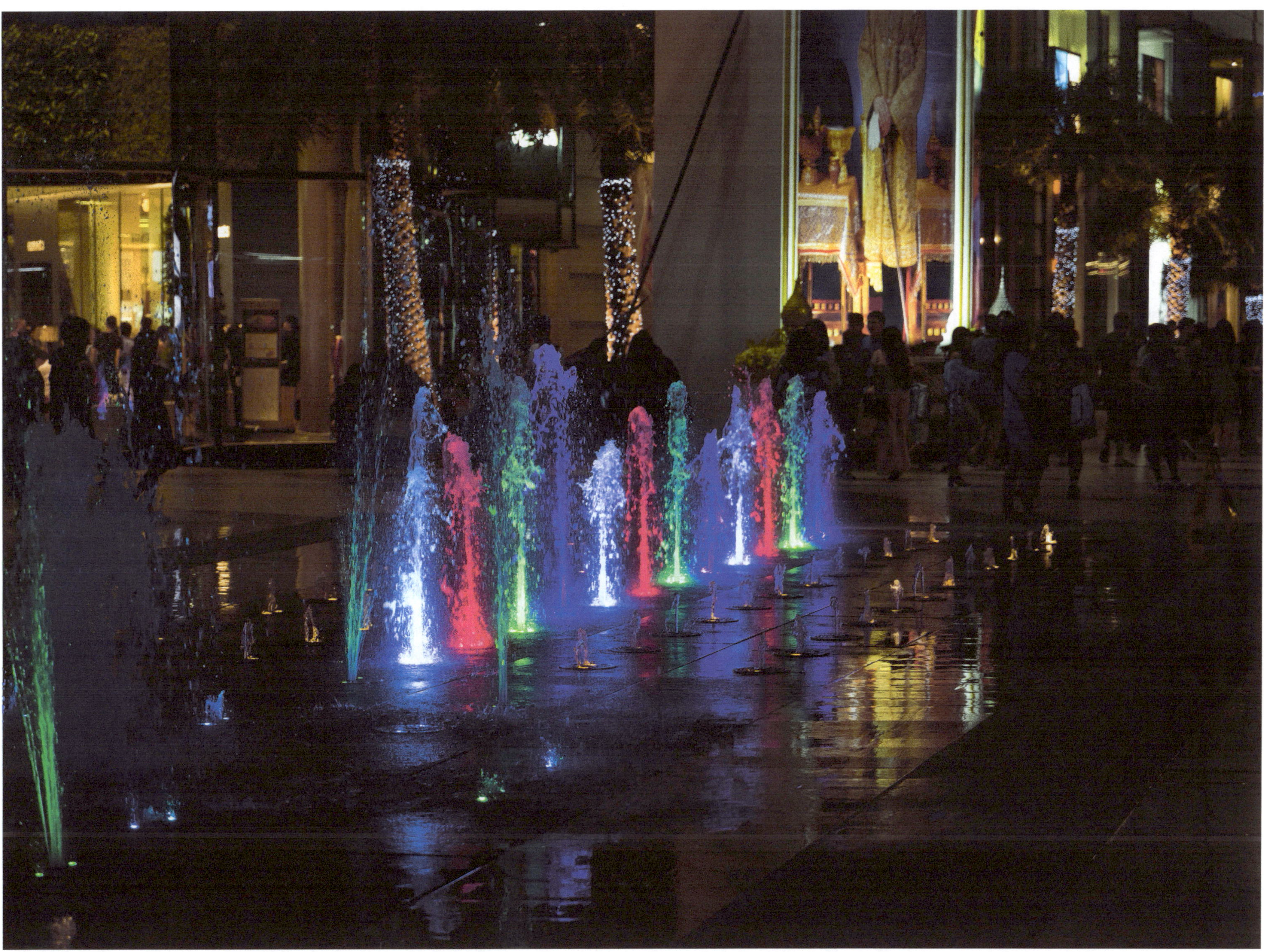

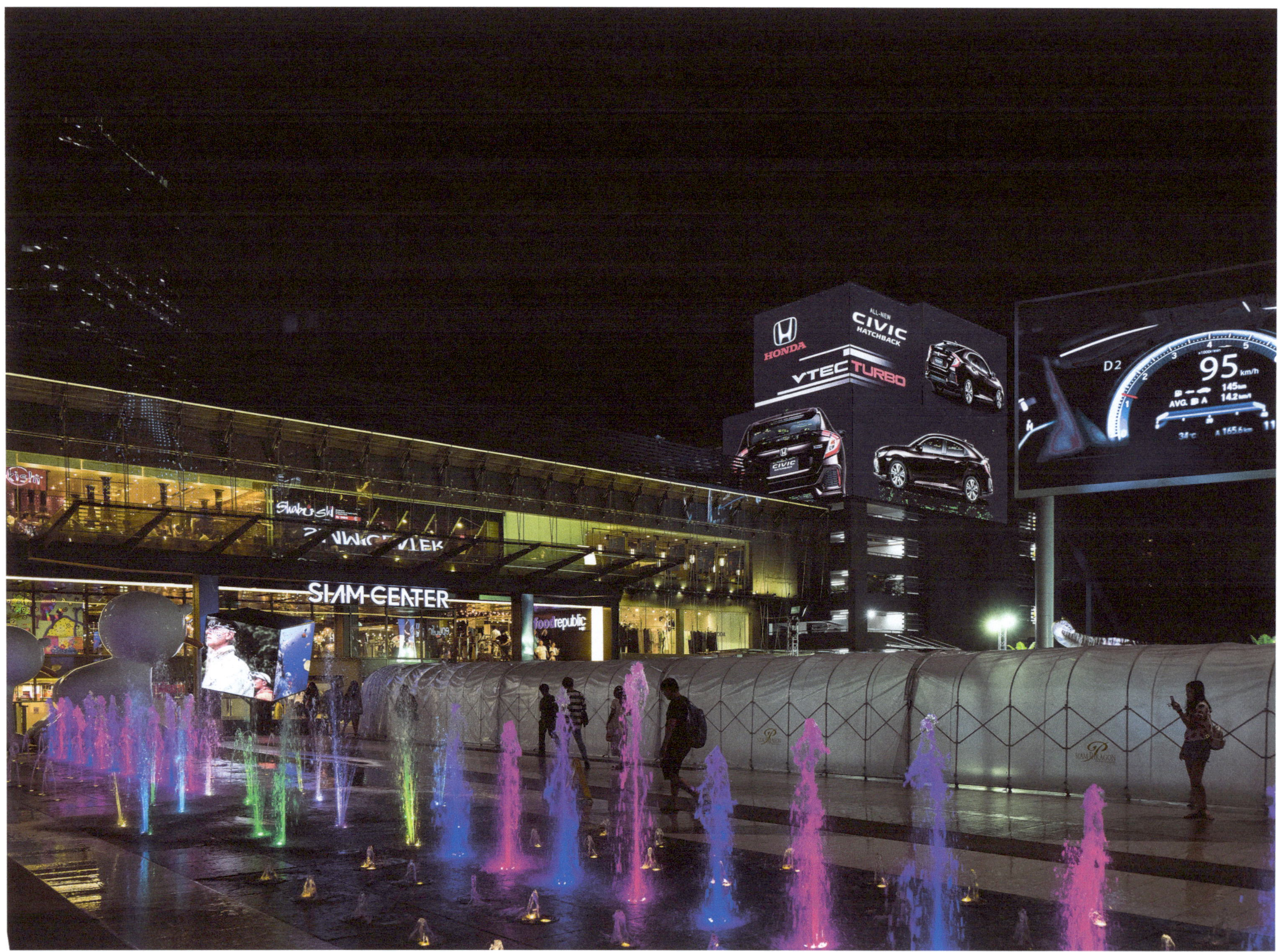
HONDA
ALL-NEW
CIVIC
HATCHBACK
VTEC TURBO
D2
95 km/h
Shabushi
SIAM CENTER
foodrepublic

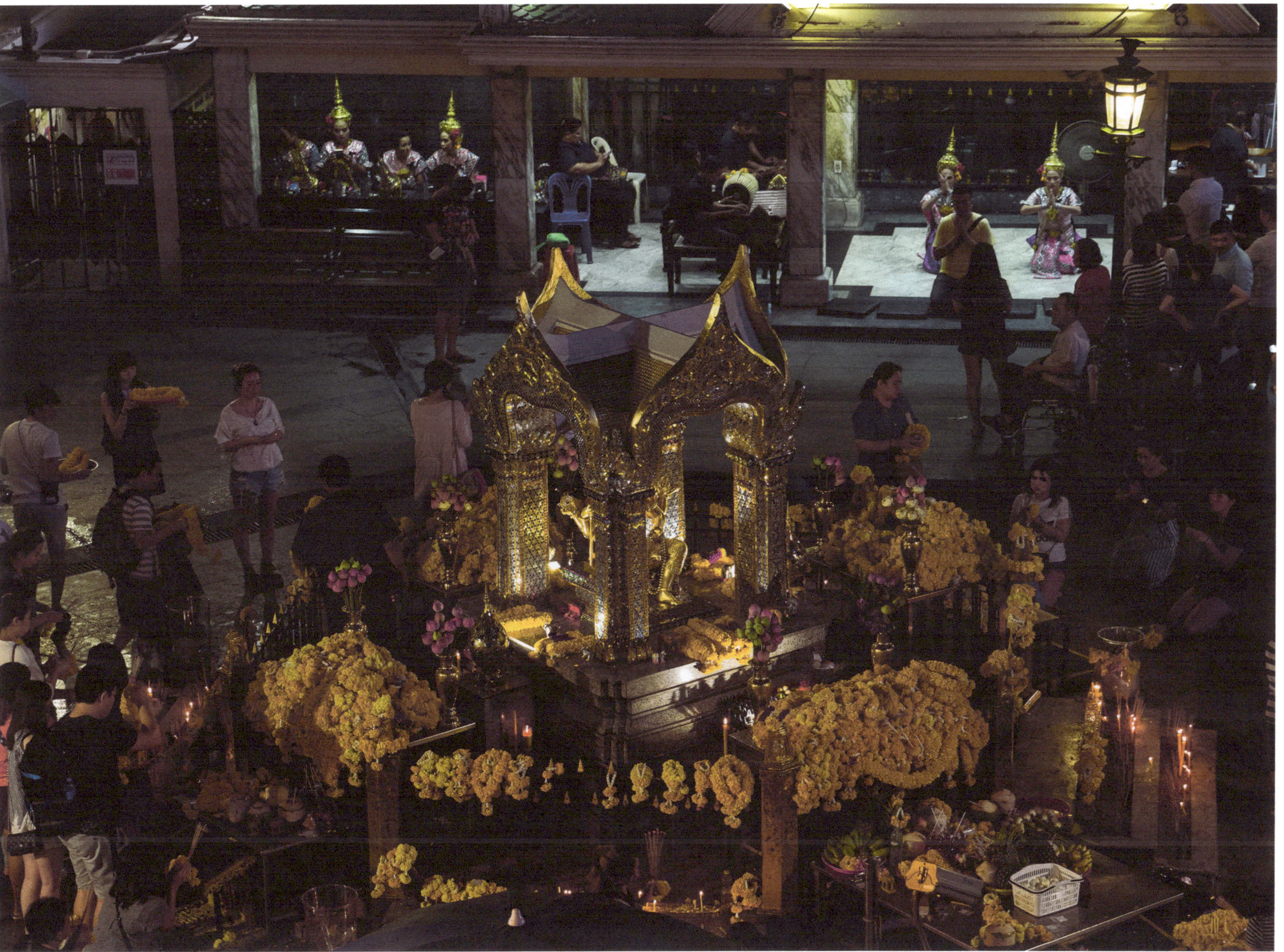

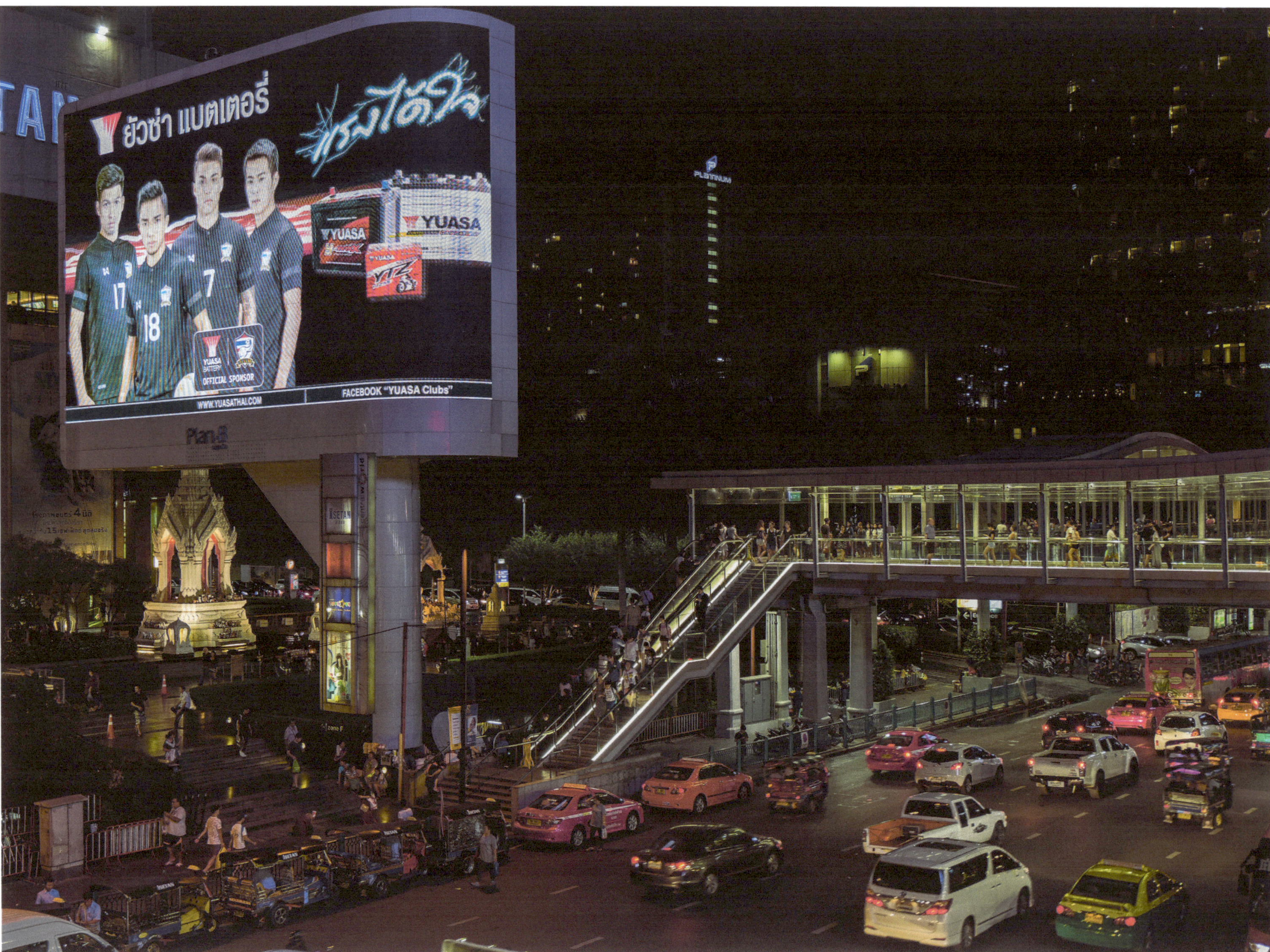
ยัวซ่า แบตเตอรี่
YUASA
YUASA
YUASA
OFFICIAL SPONSOR
WWW.YUASATHAI.COM
FACEBOOK "YUASA Clubs"
PLATINUM

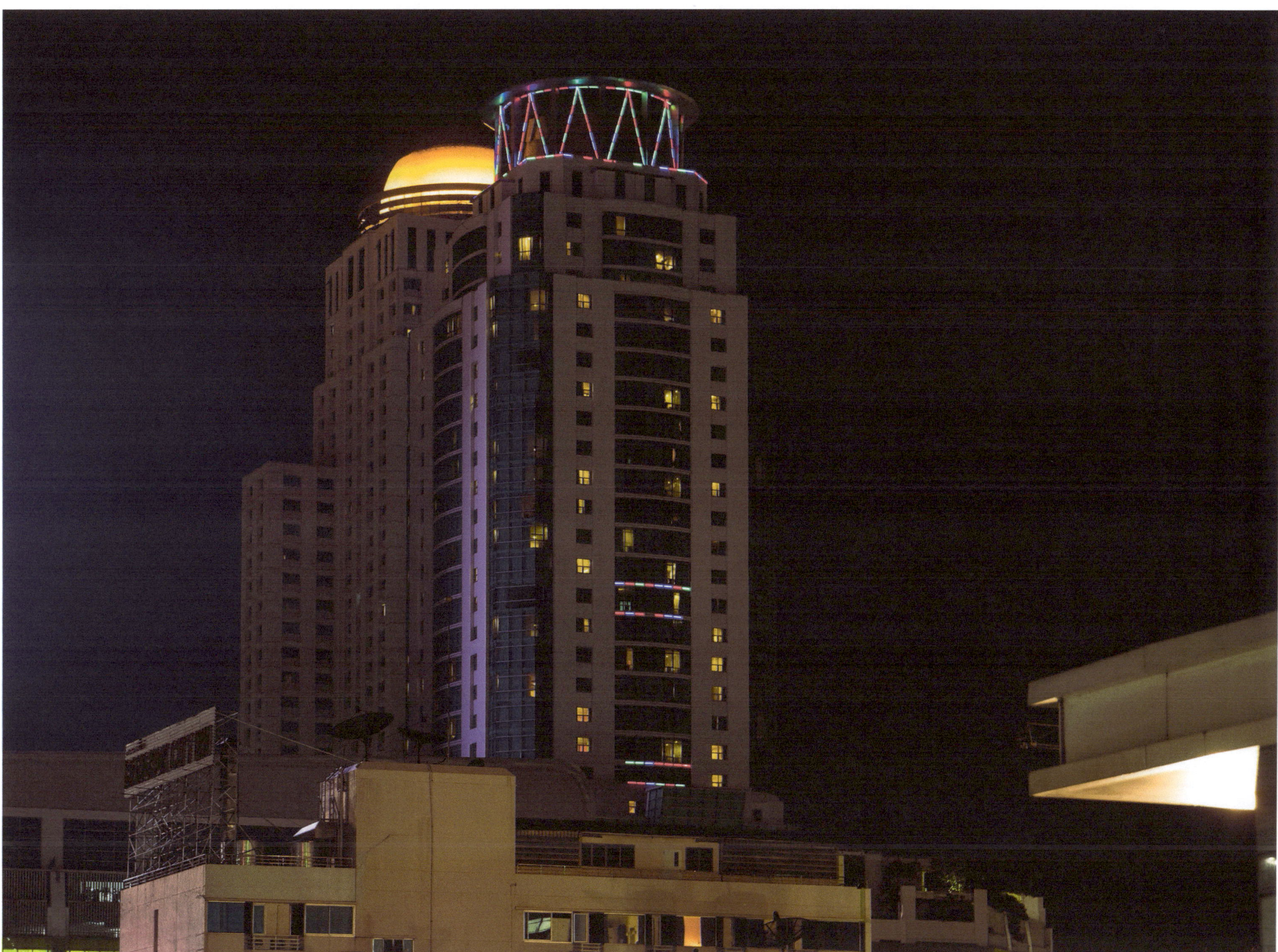

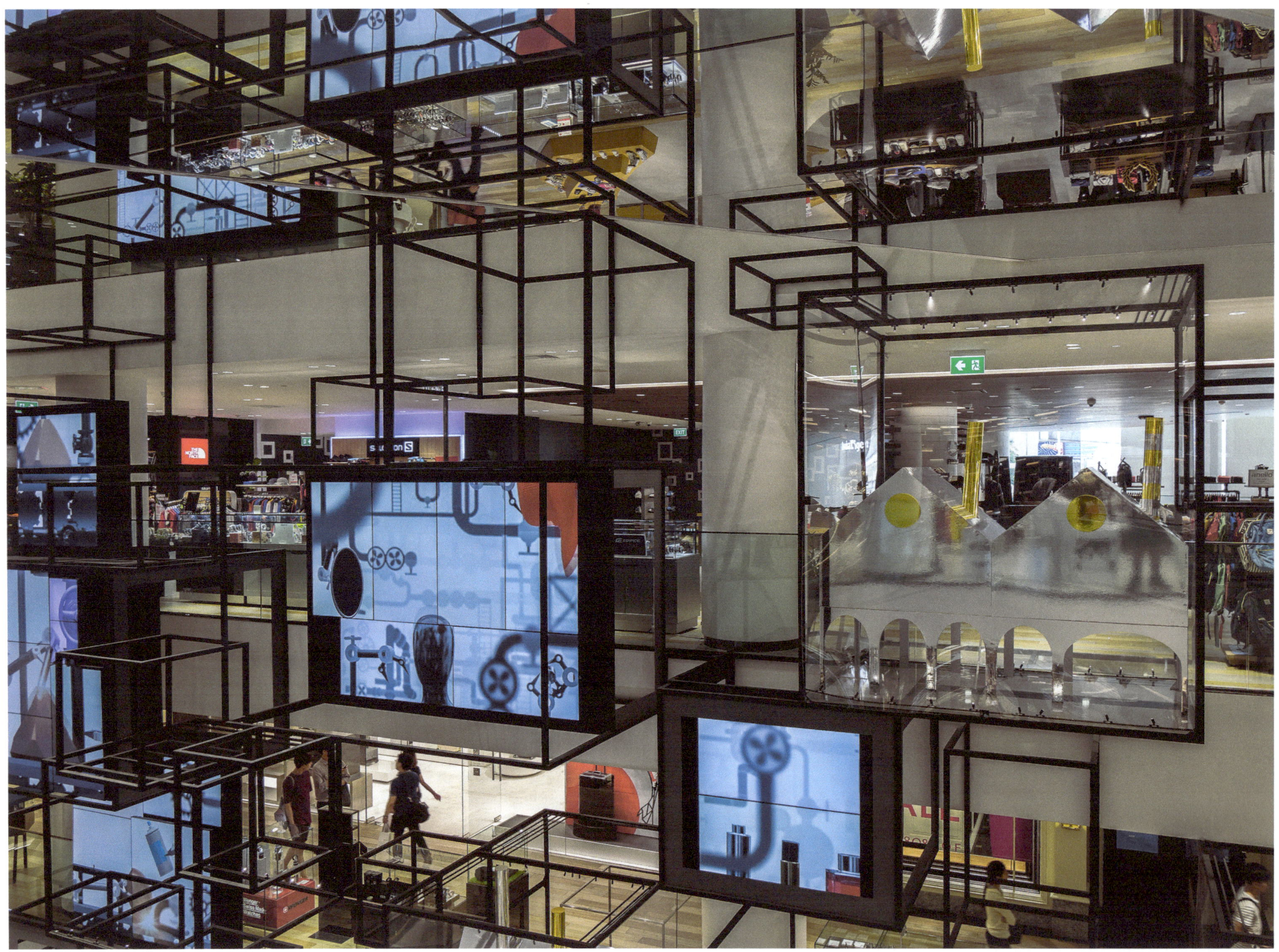

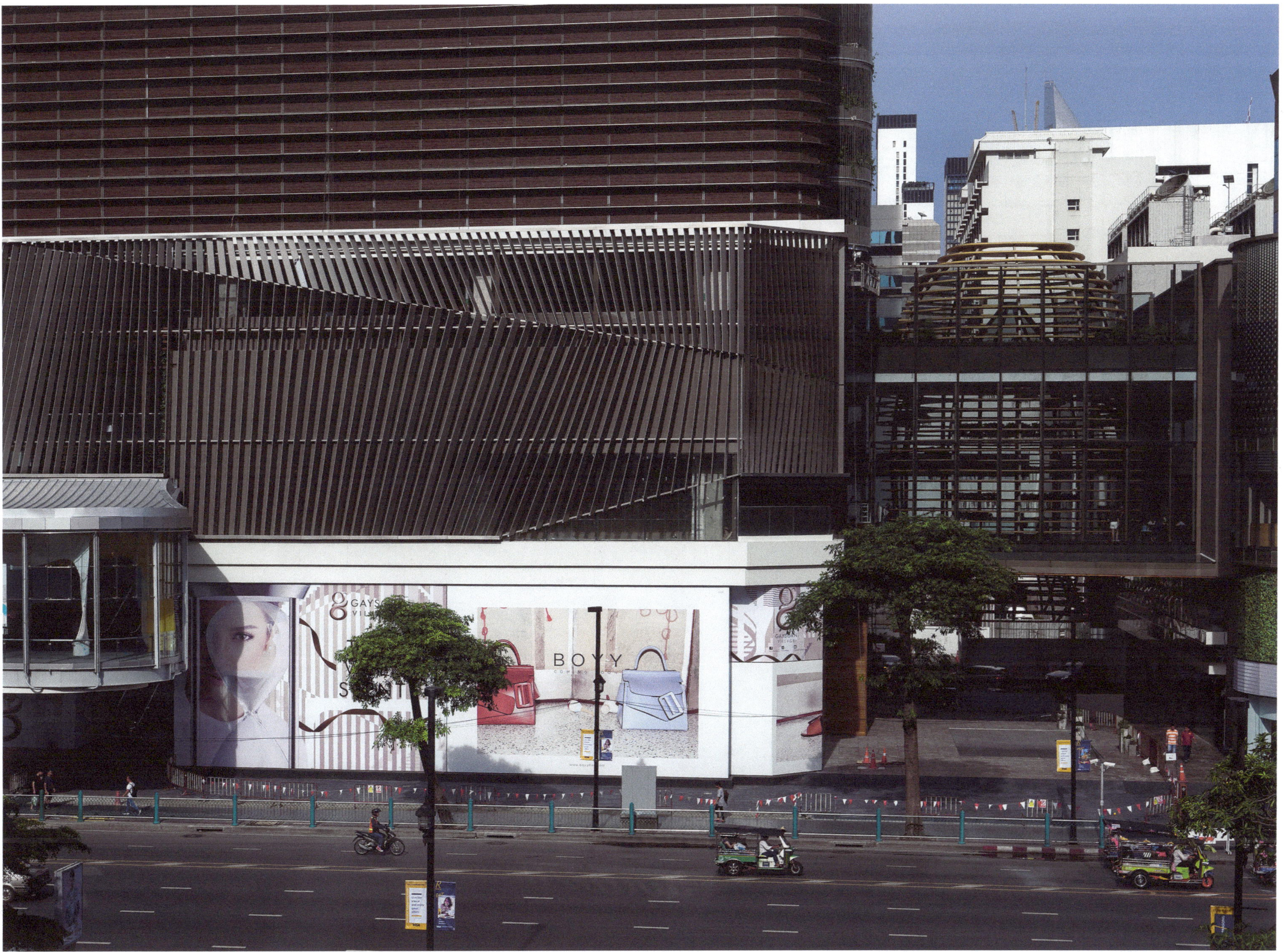
BOYY

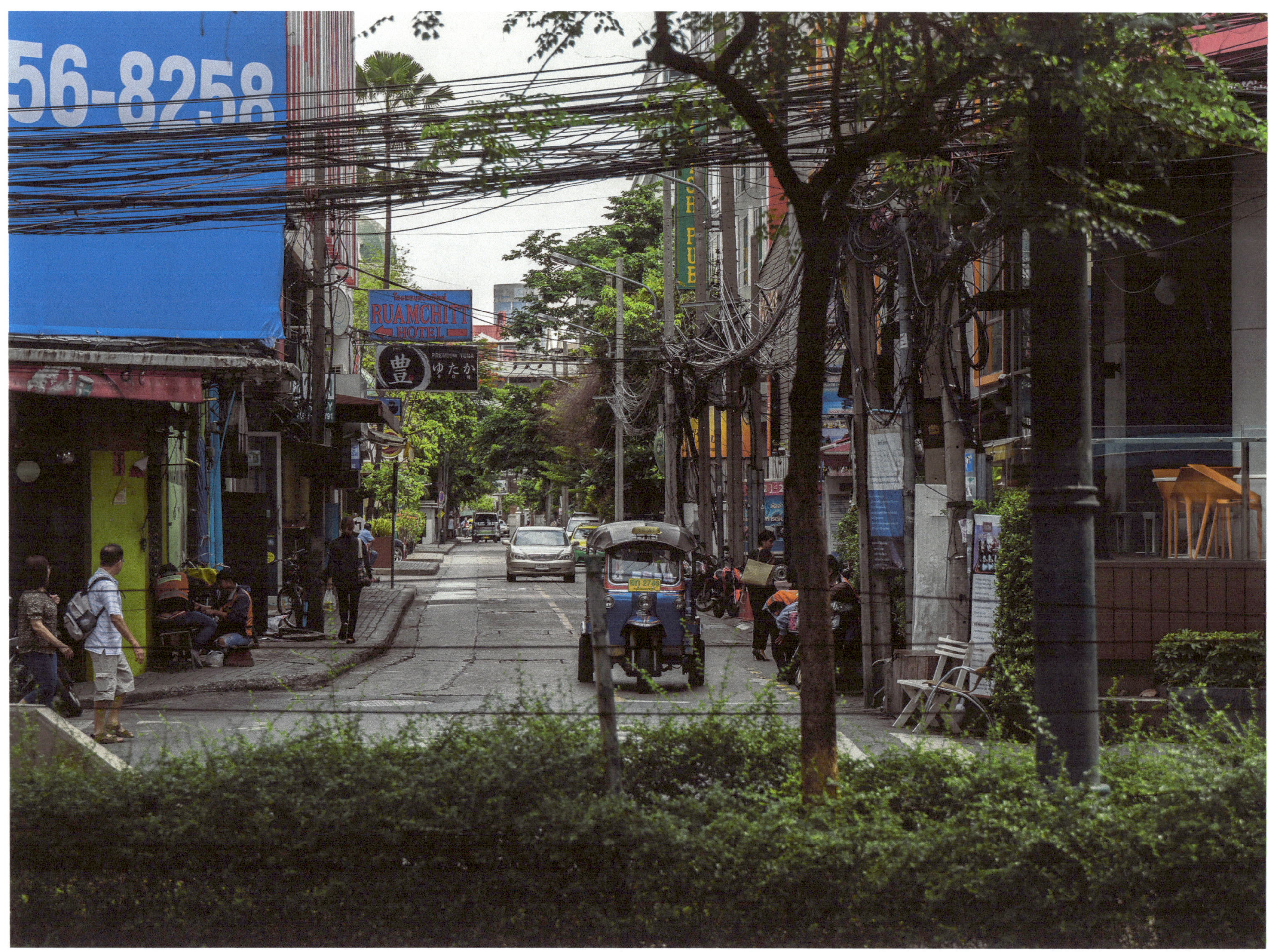
56-8258
RUAMCHITT
HOTEL
豊
PREMIUM TUNA
ゆたか

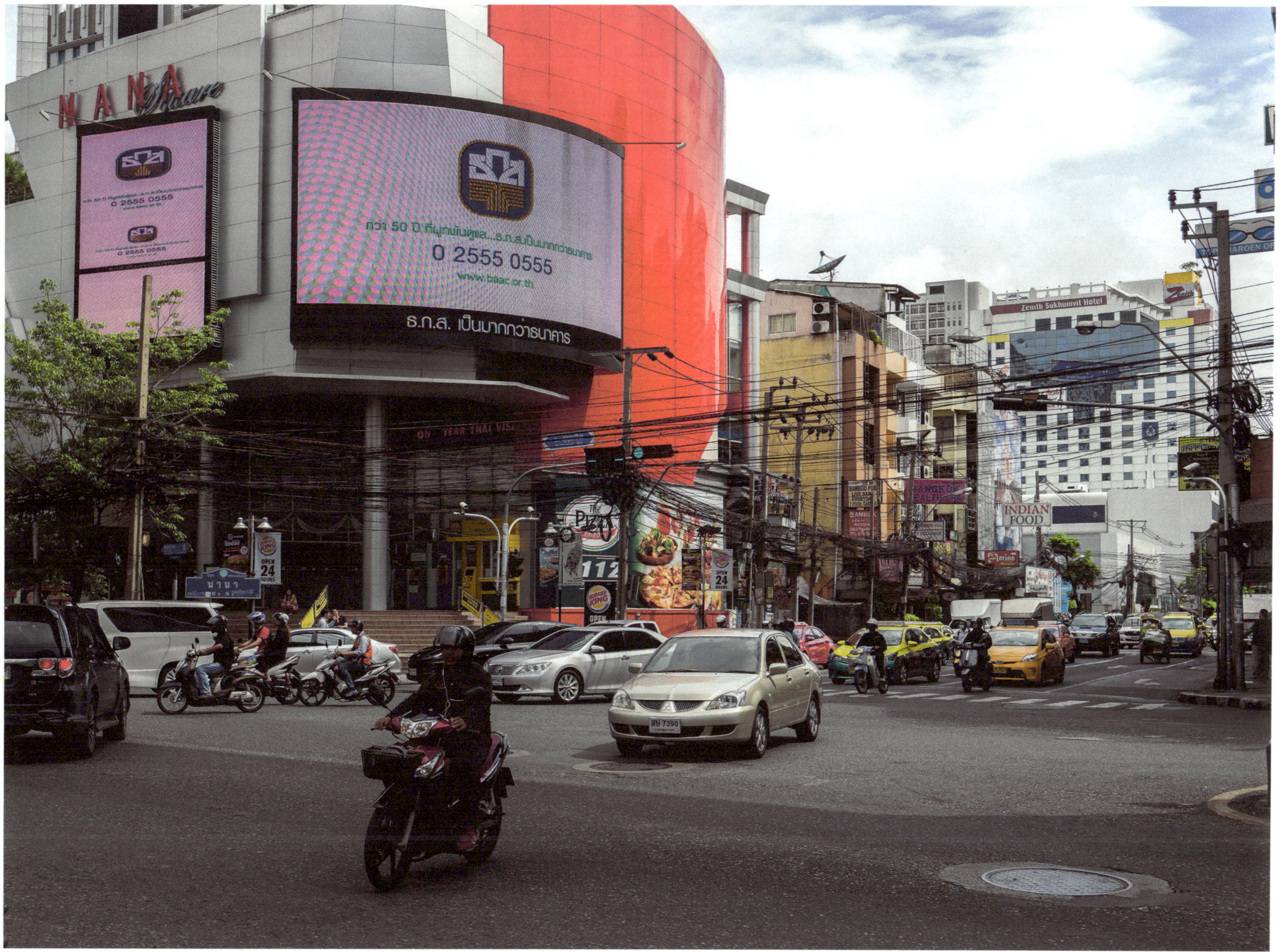
NANA
0 2555 0555
www.baac.or.th
ธ.ก.ส. เป็นมากกว่าธนาคาร
Zenith Sukhumvit Hotel
INDIAN FOOD
OPEN 24 HOURS
112

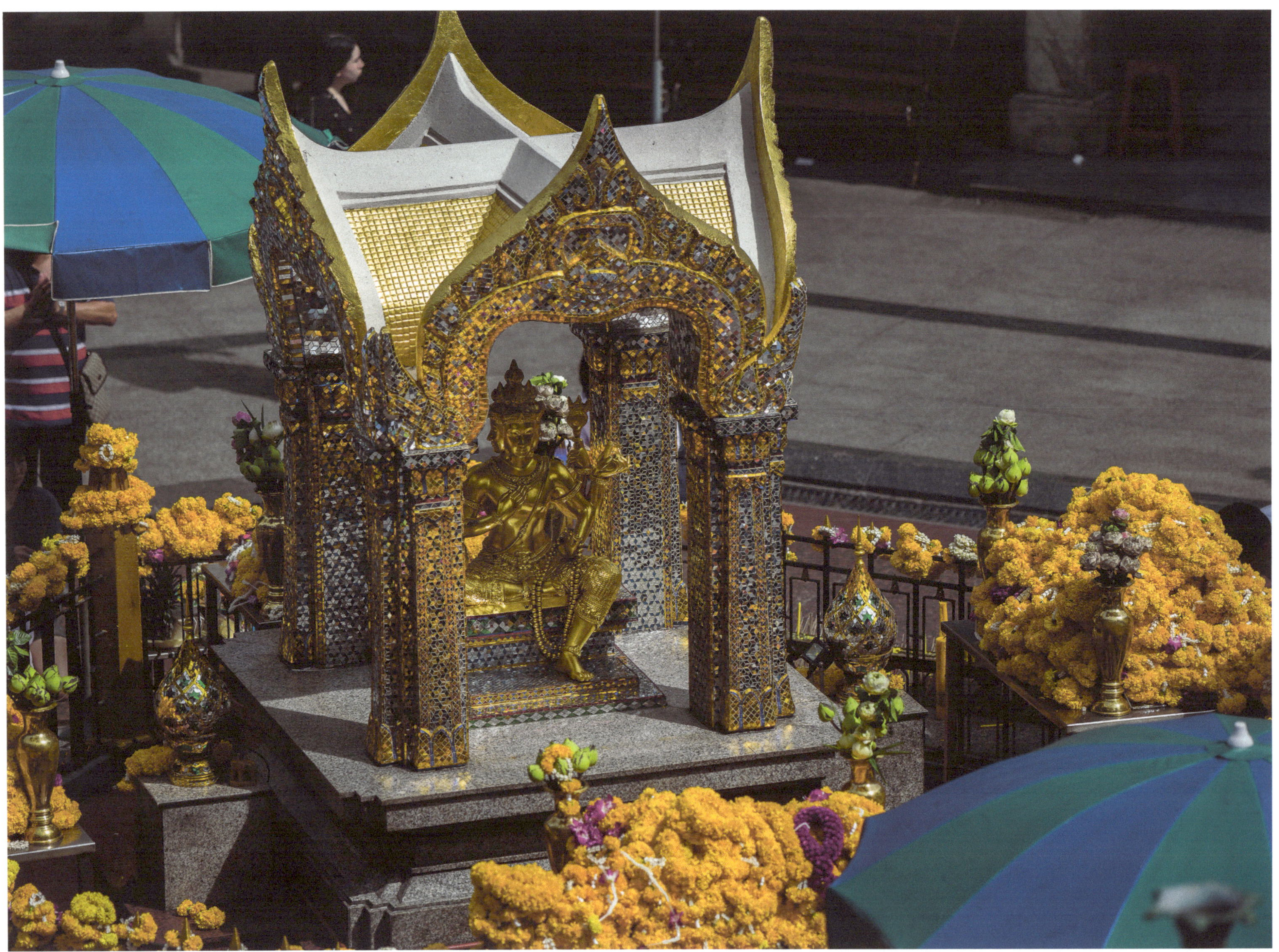

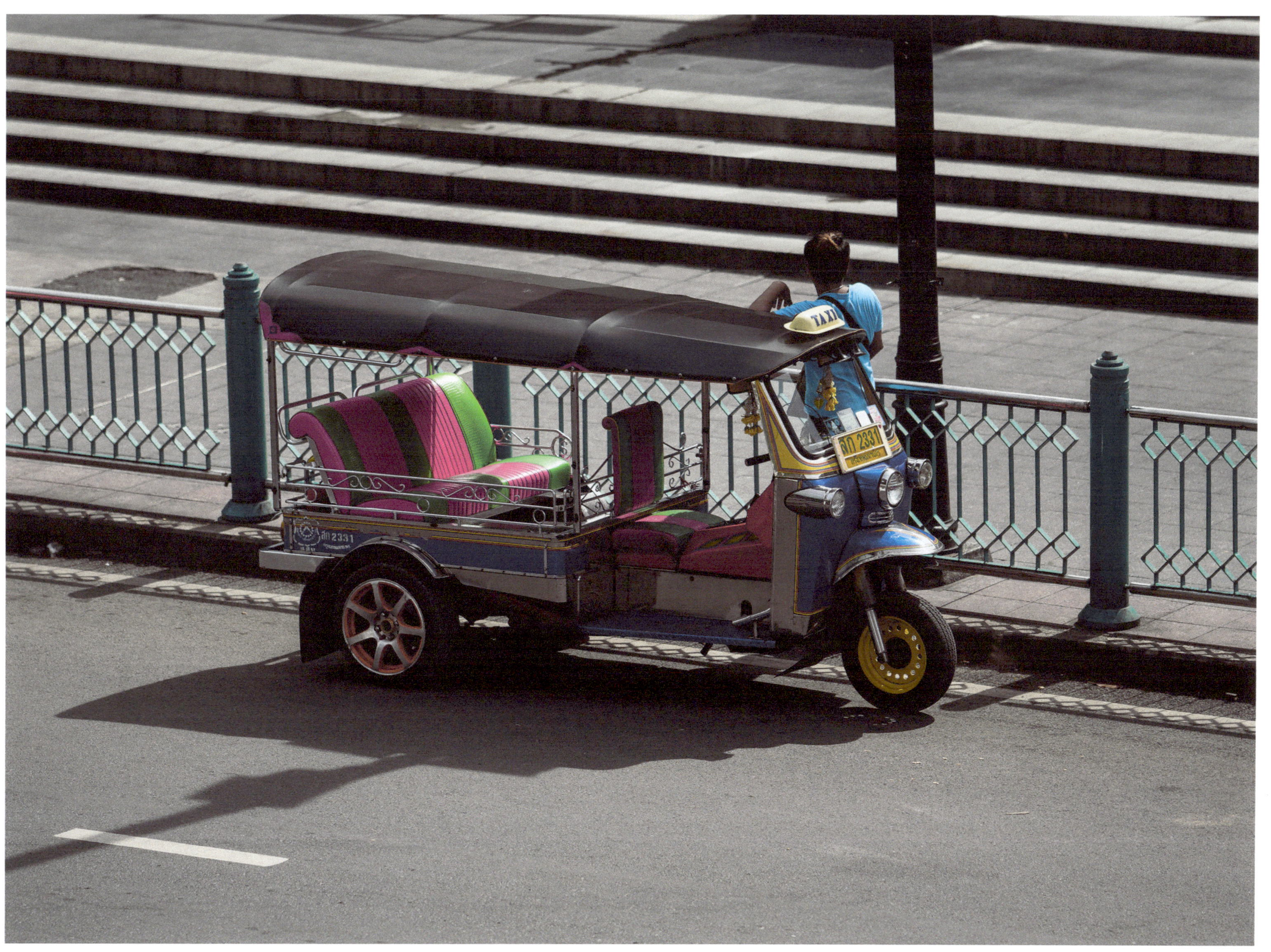
TAXI
2331

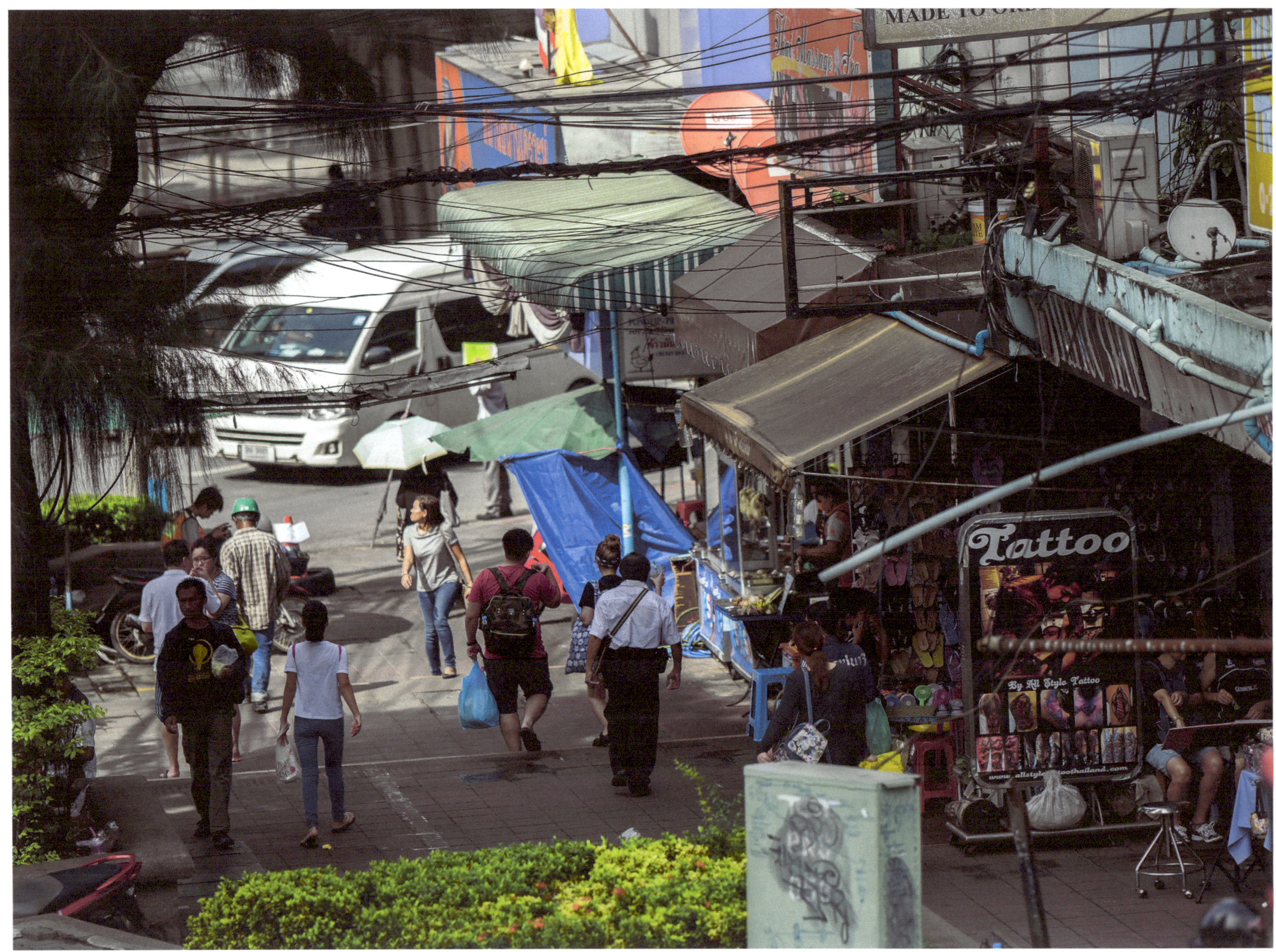
MADE TO
Tattoo
By All Style Tattoo

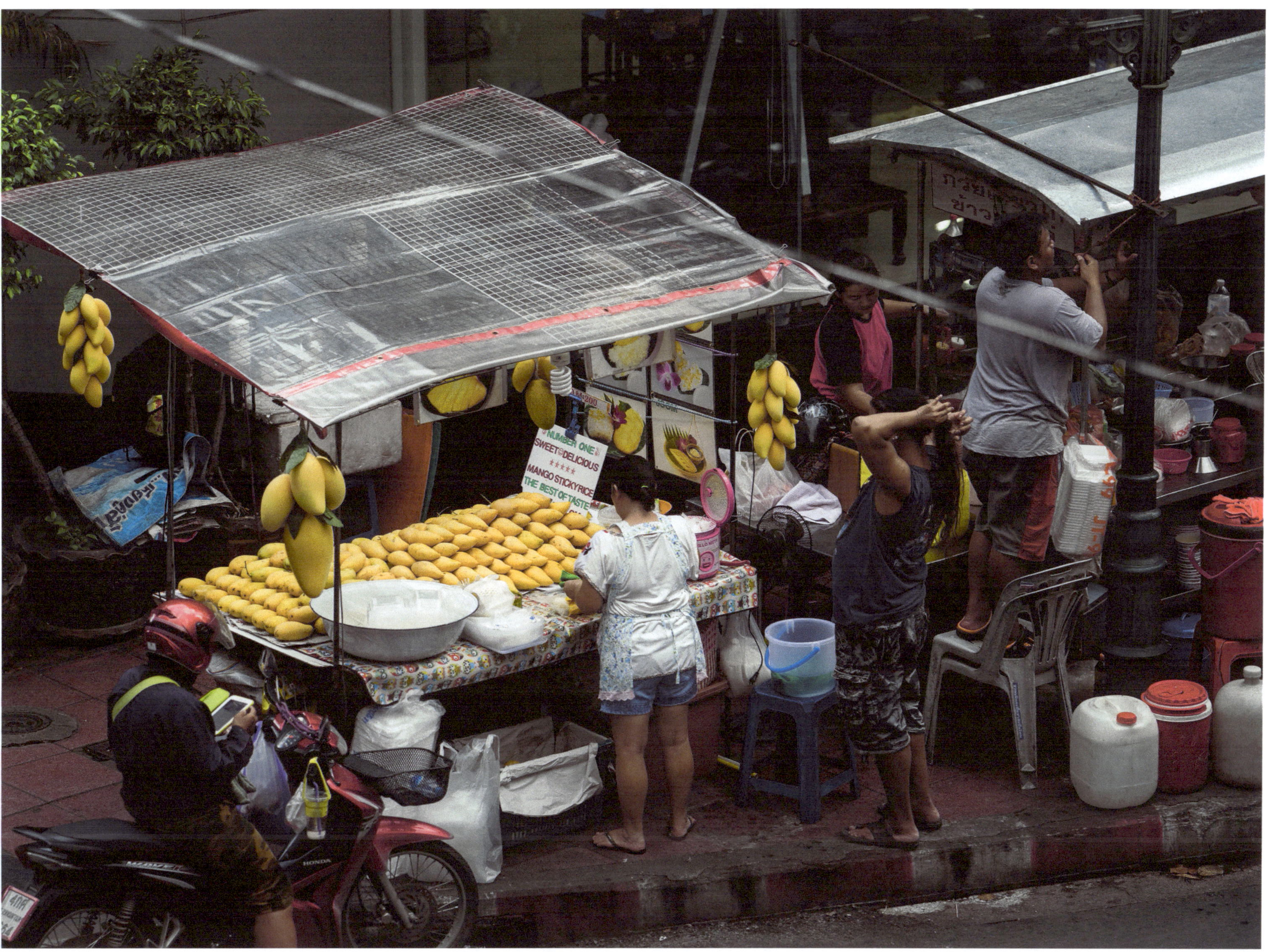
NUMBER ONE
SWEET DELICIOUS
*****
MANGO STICKY RICE
THE BEST OF TASTE

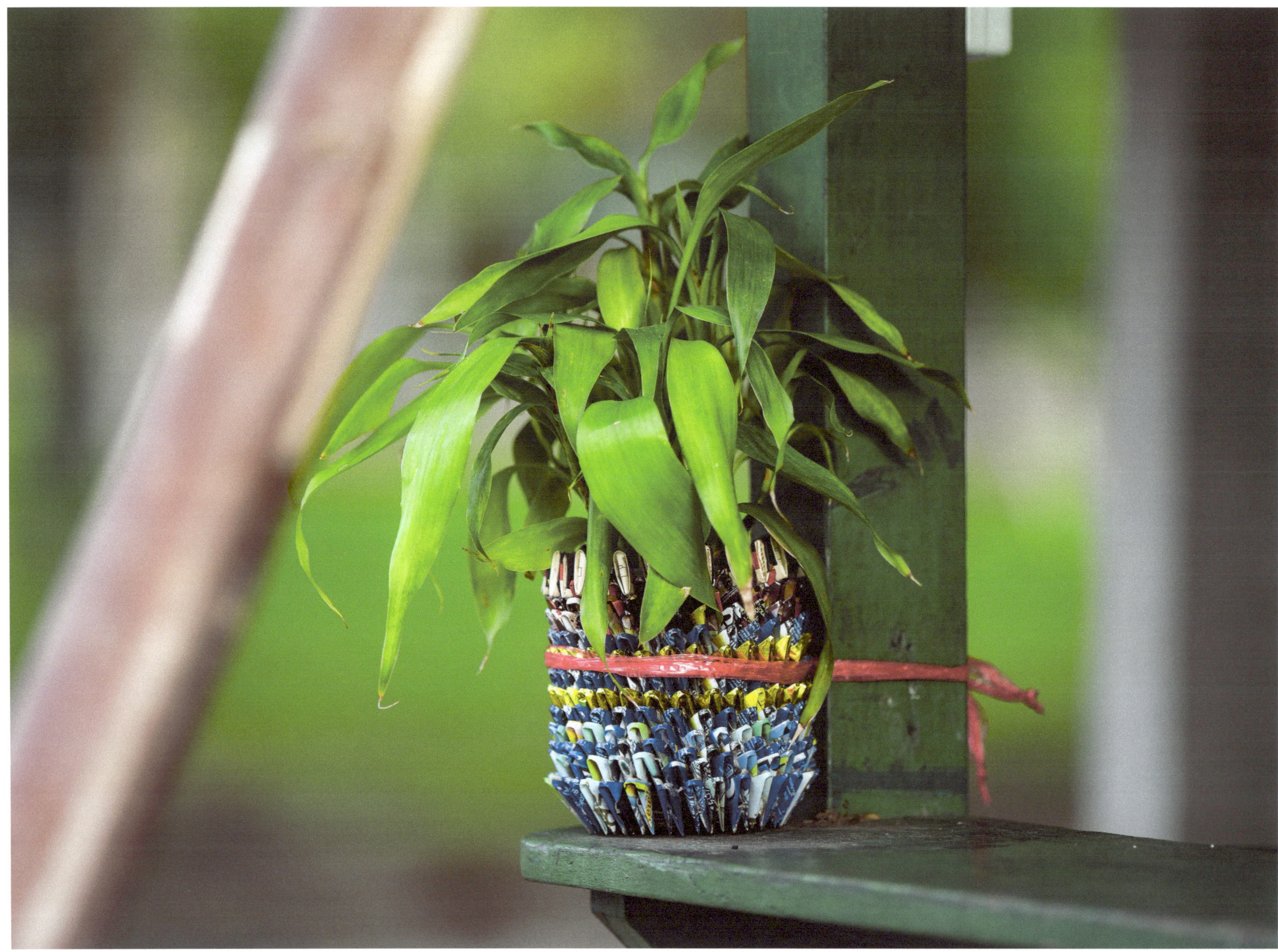

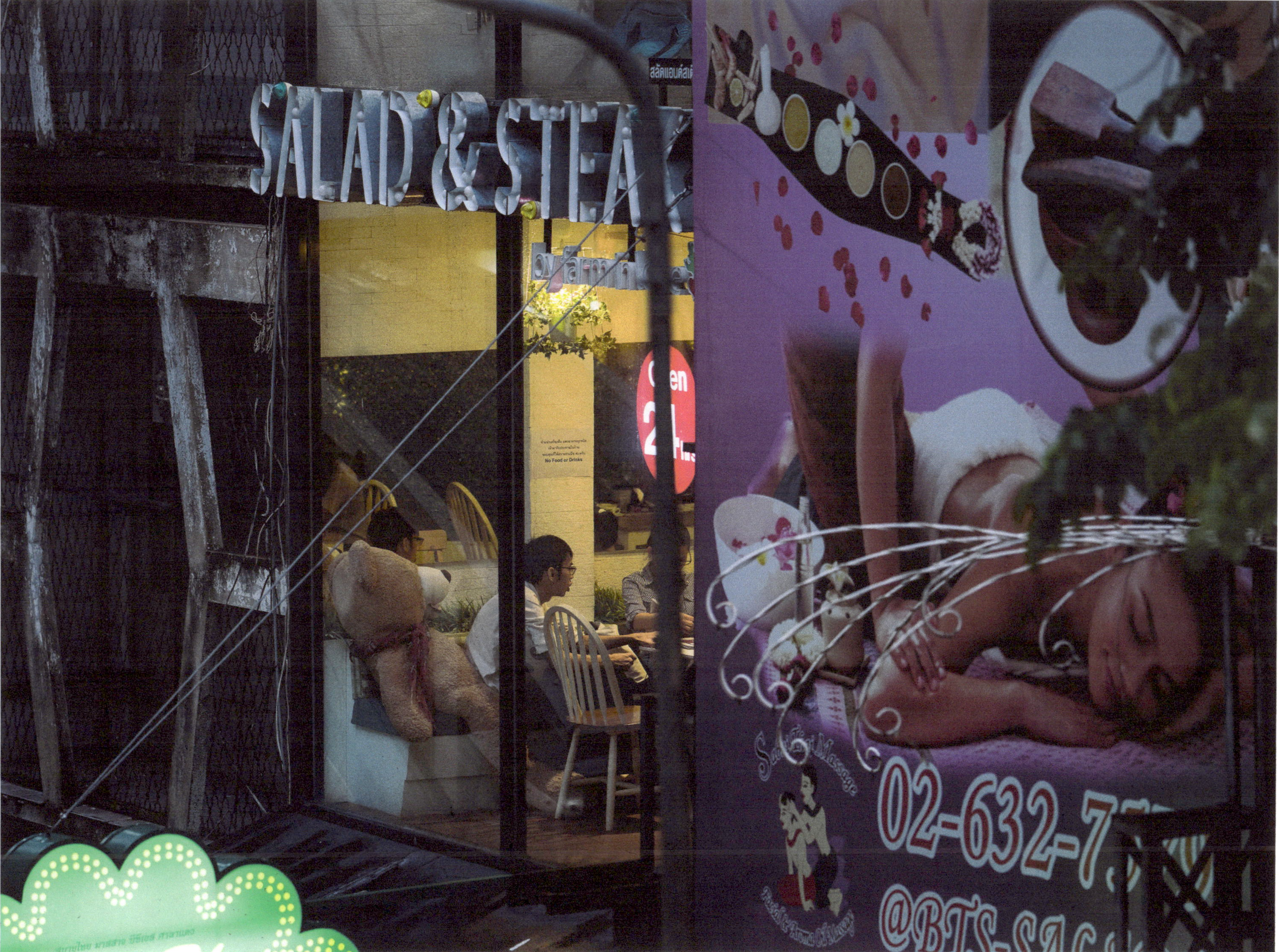
SALAD & STEA
02-632-7

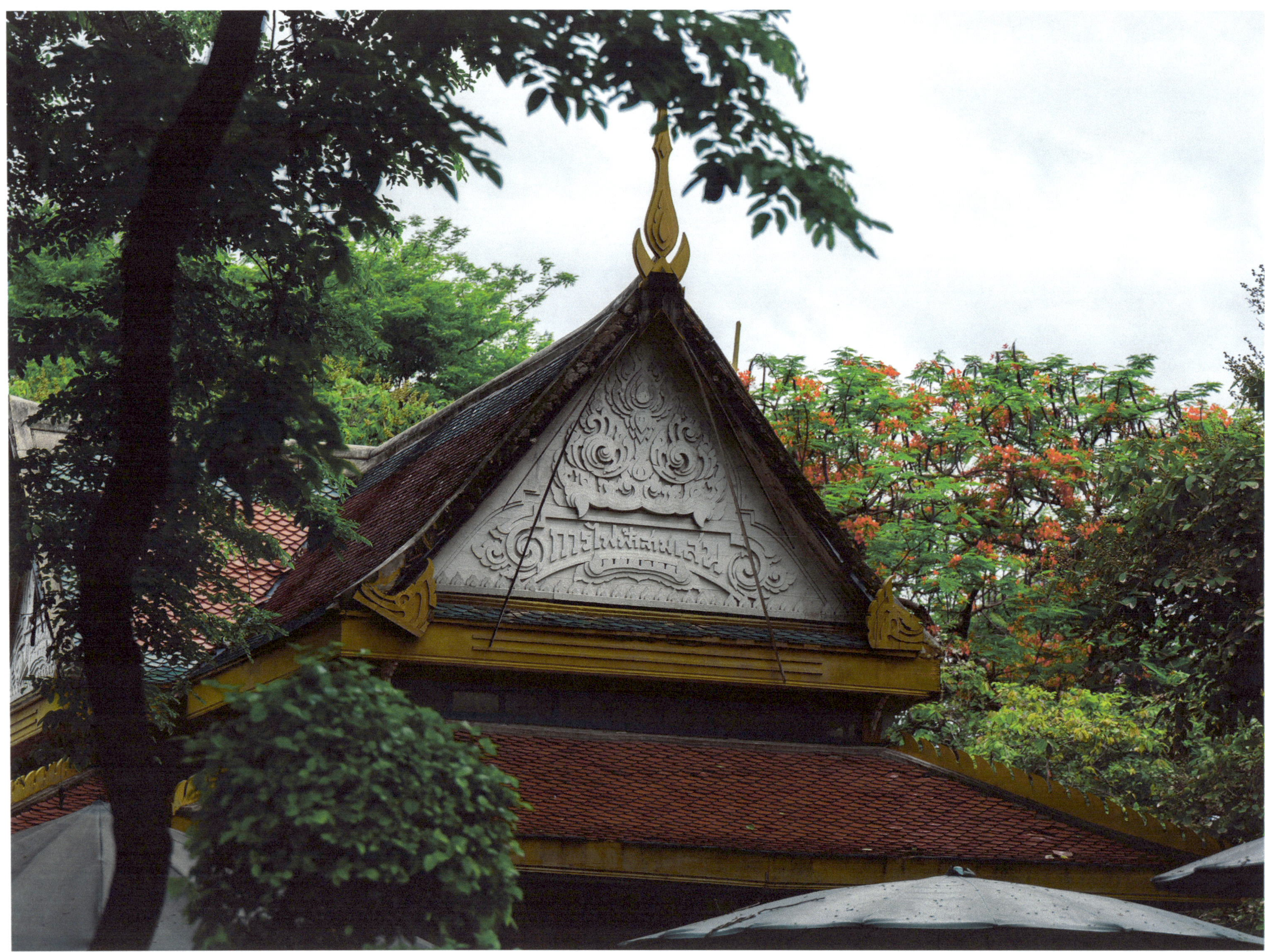
การไฟฟ้าสามเสน

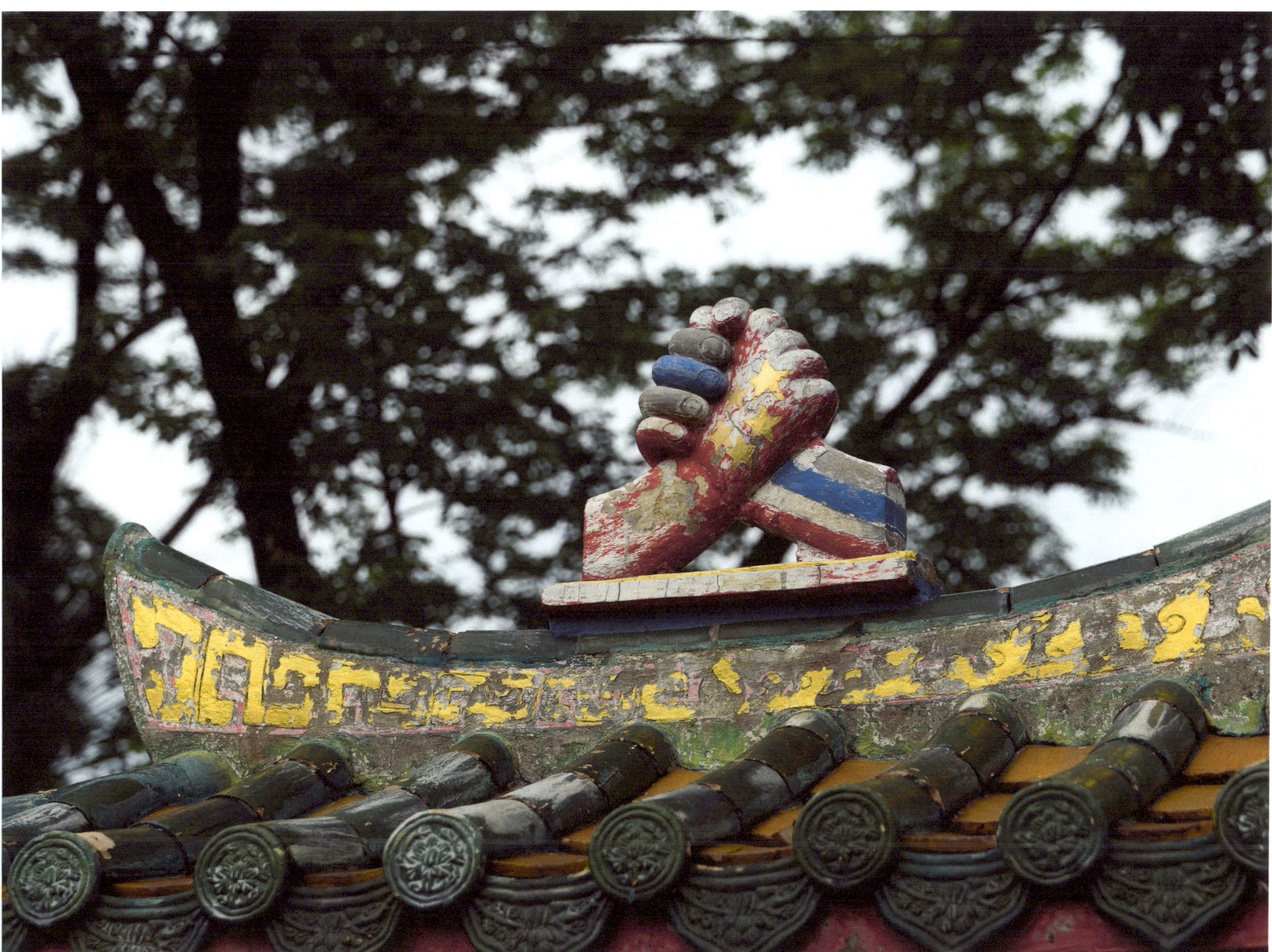

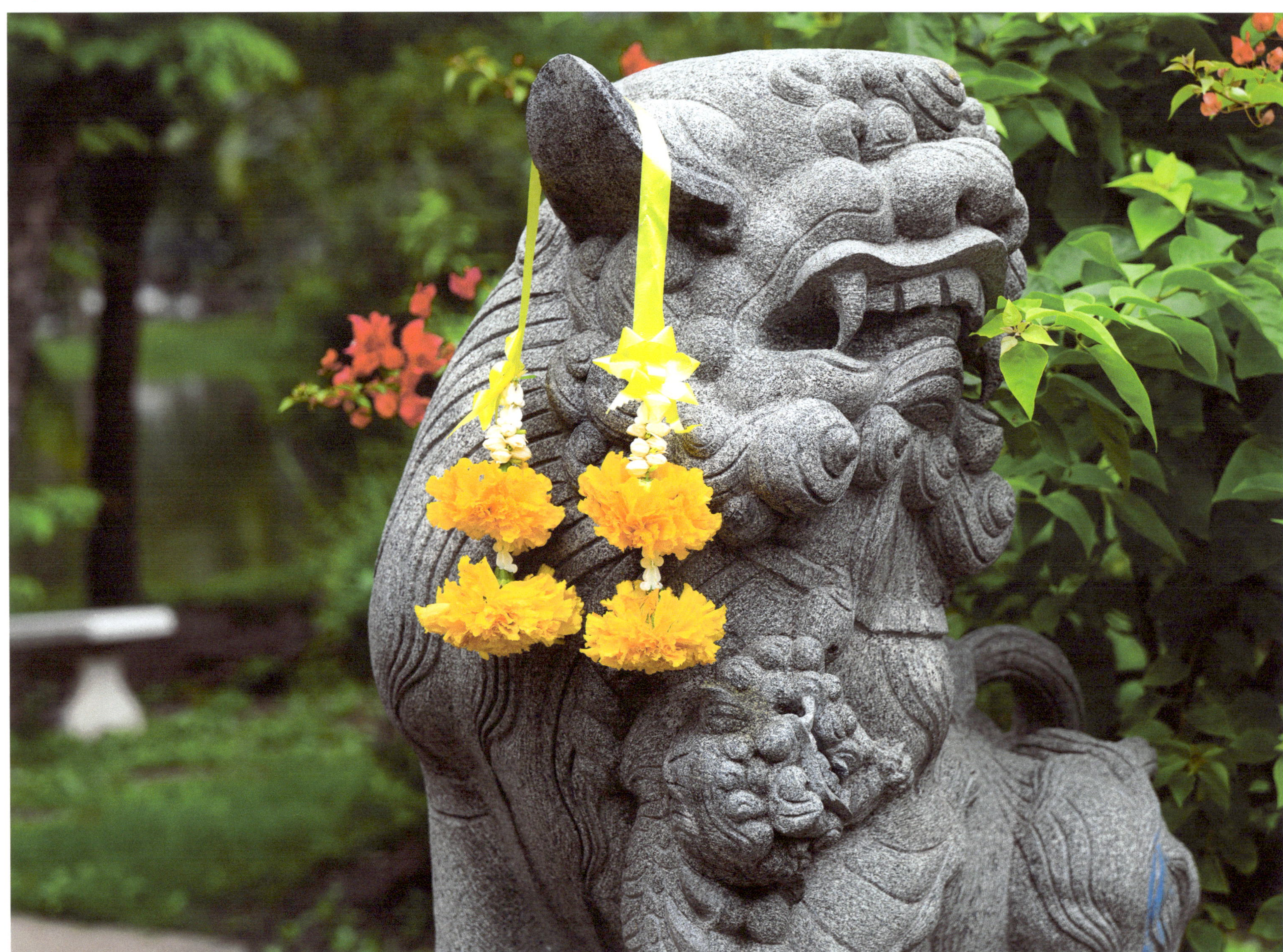

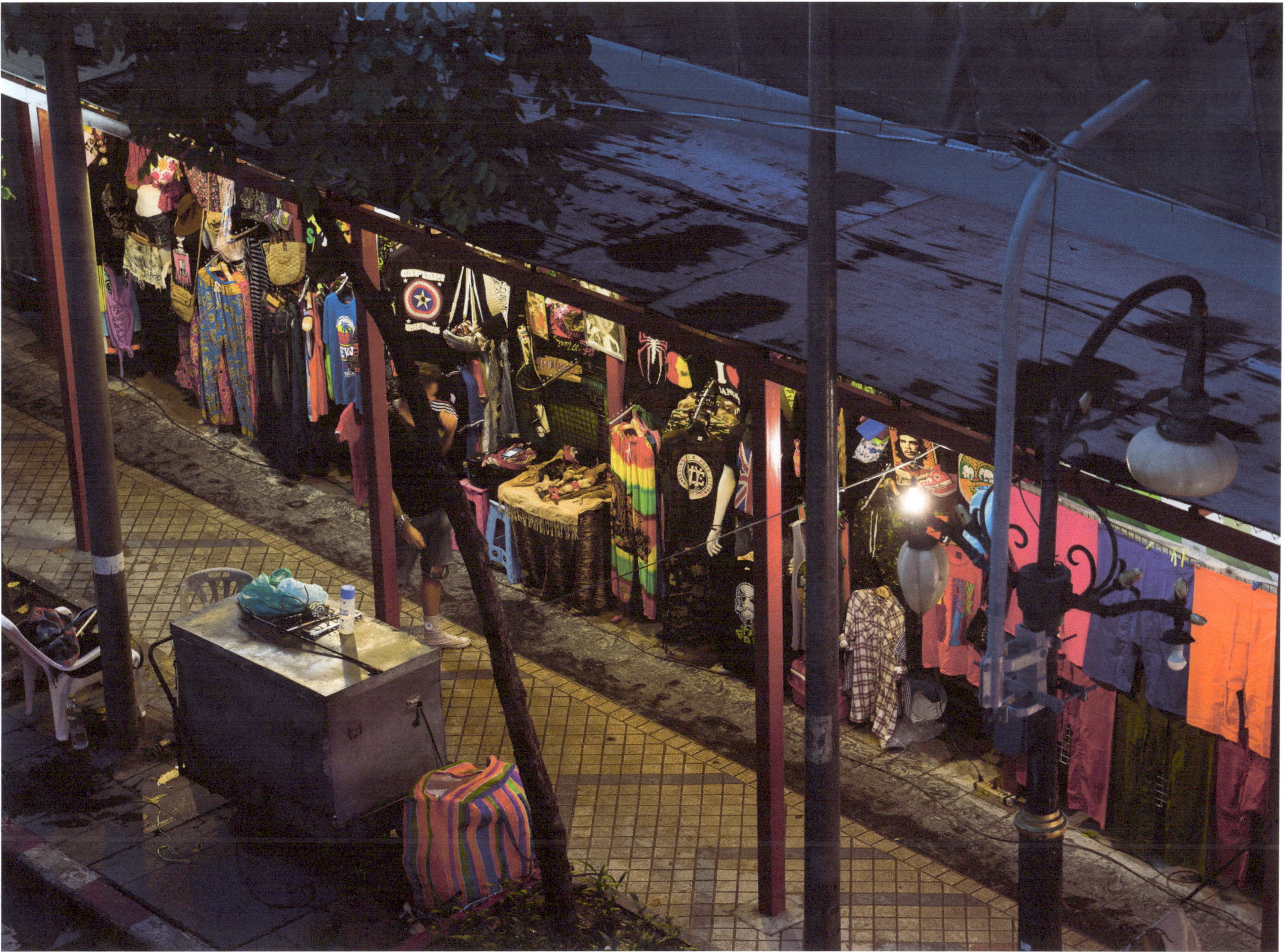

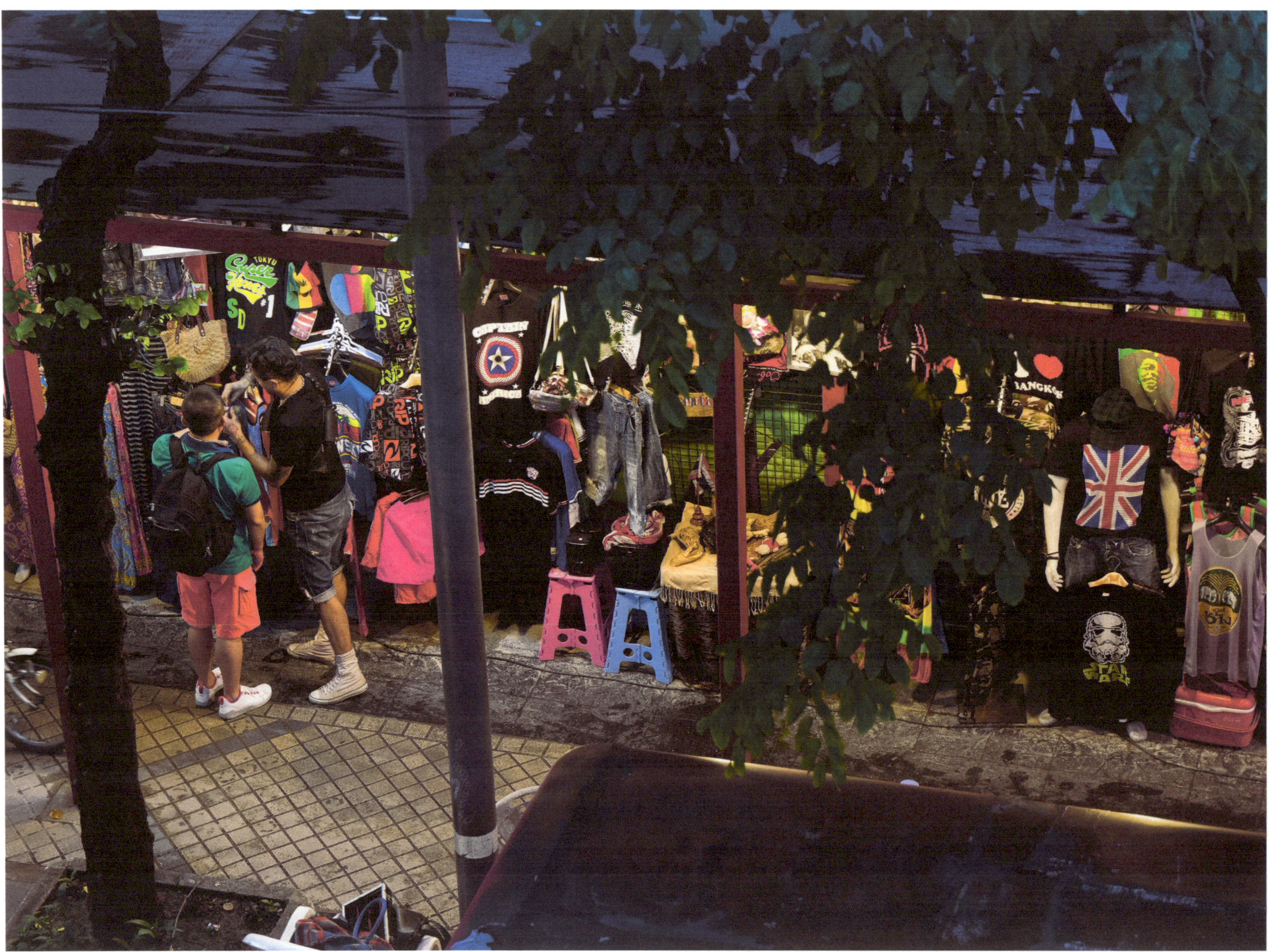
TOKYU
#1
SD
STAR
WARS

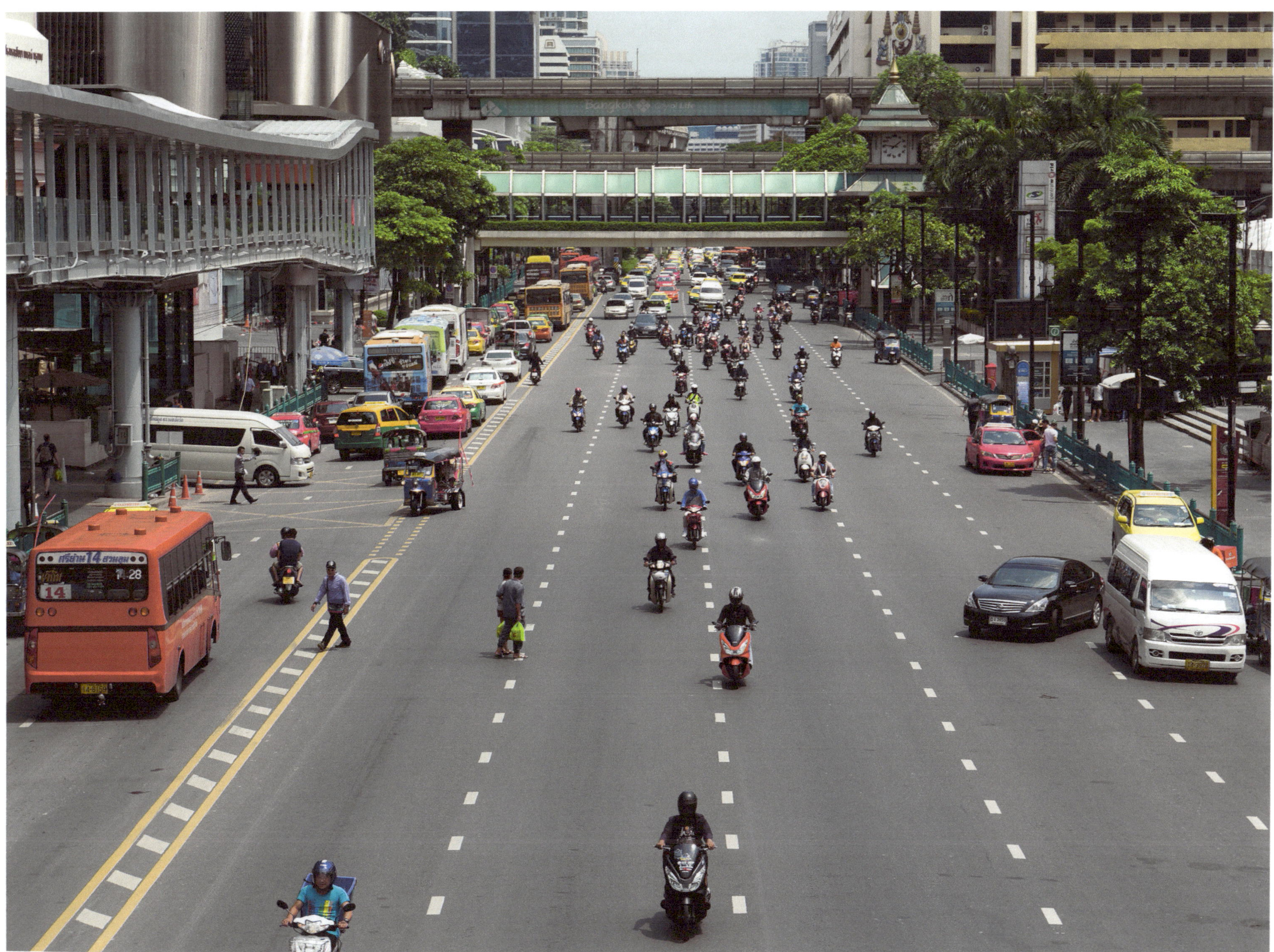
Bangkok
14

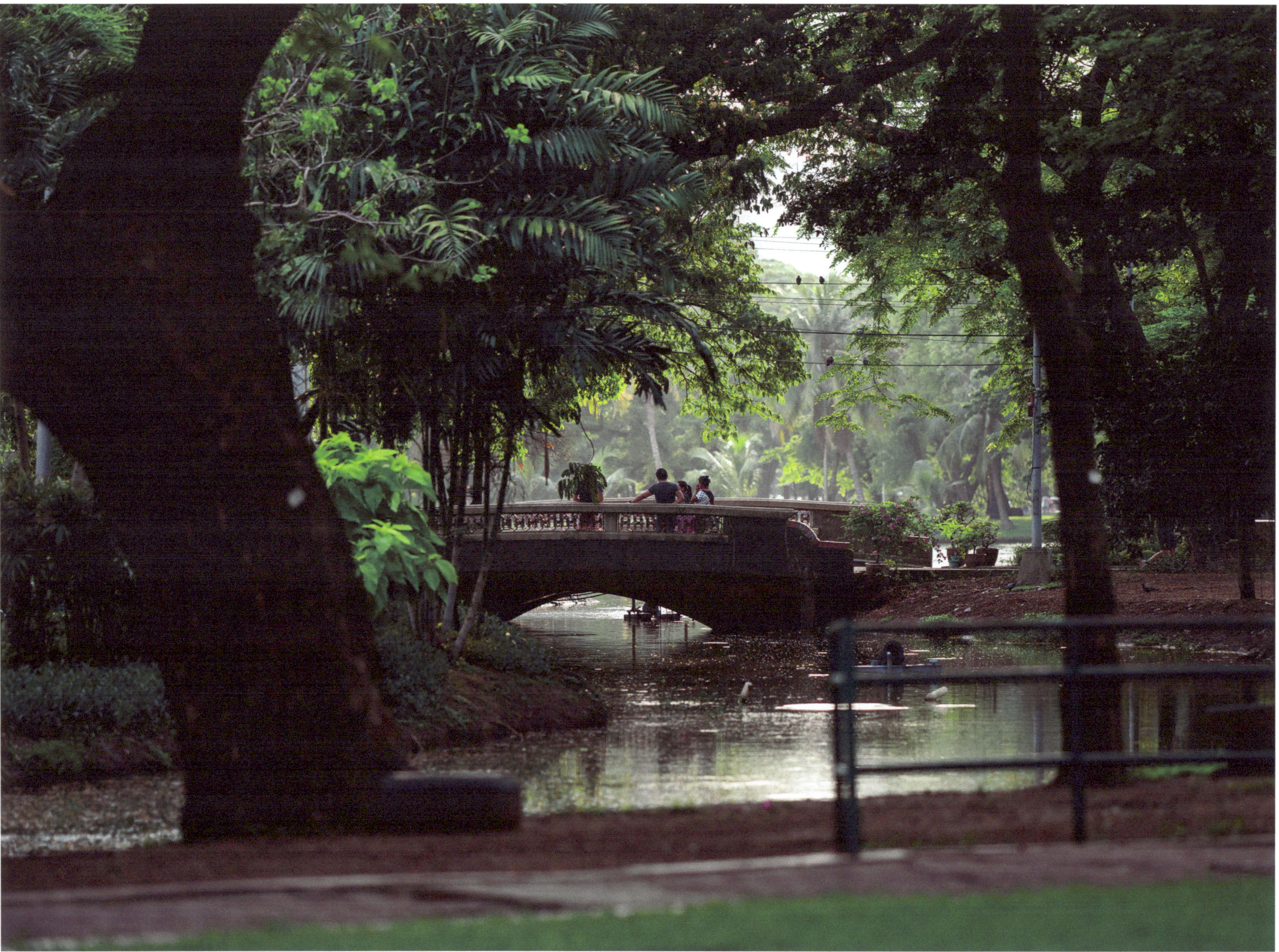

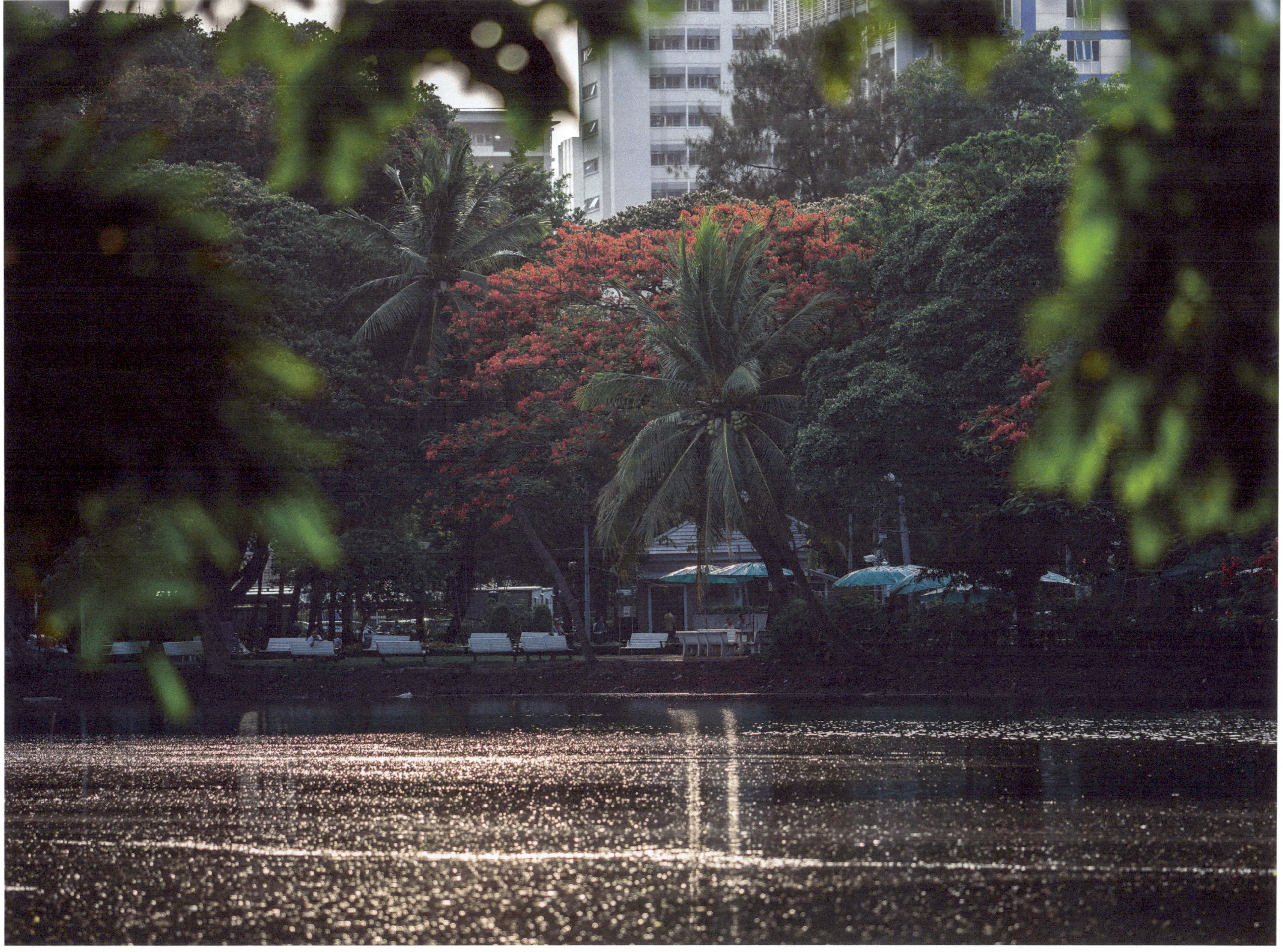

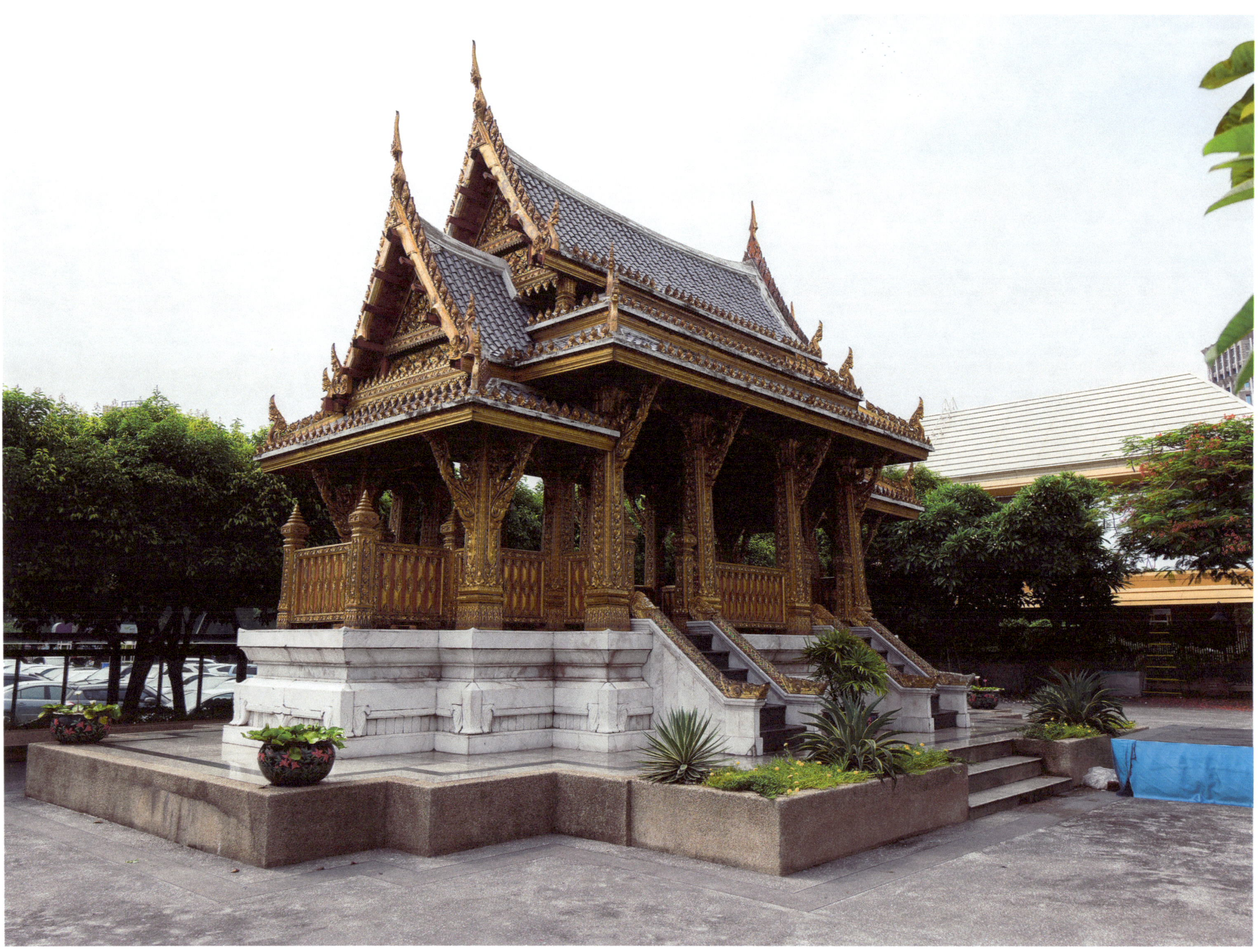

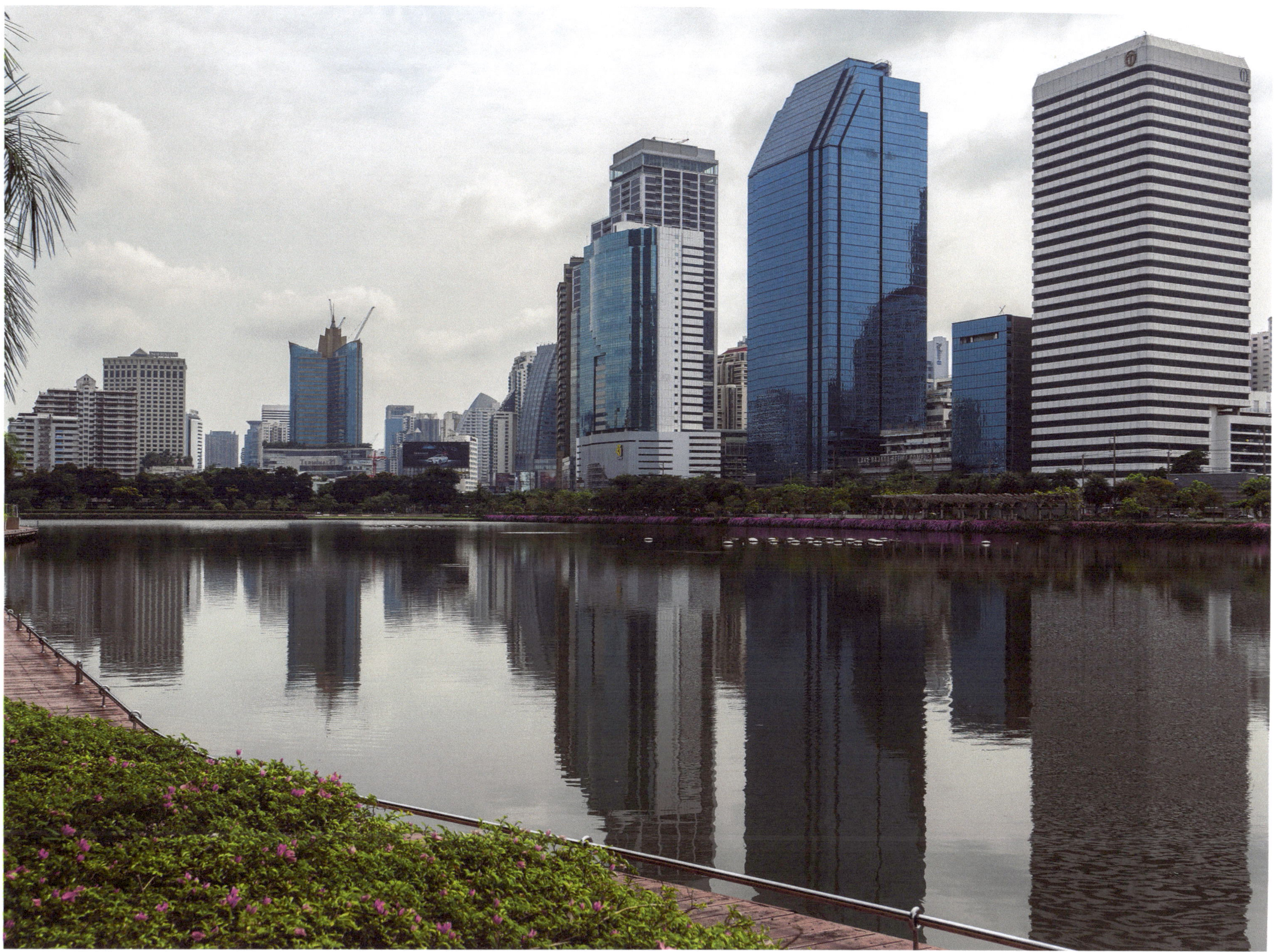

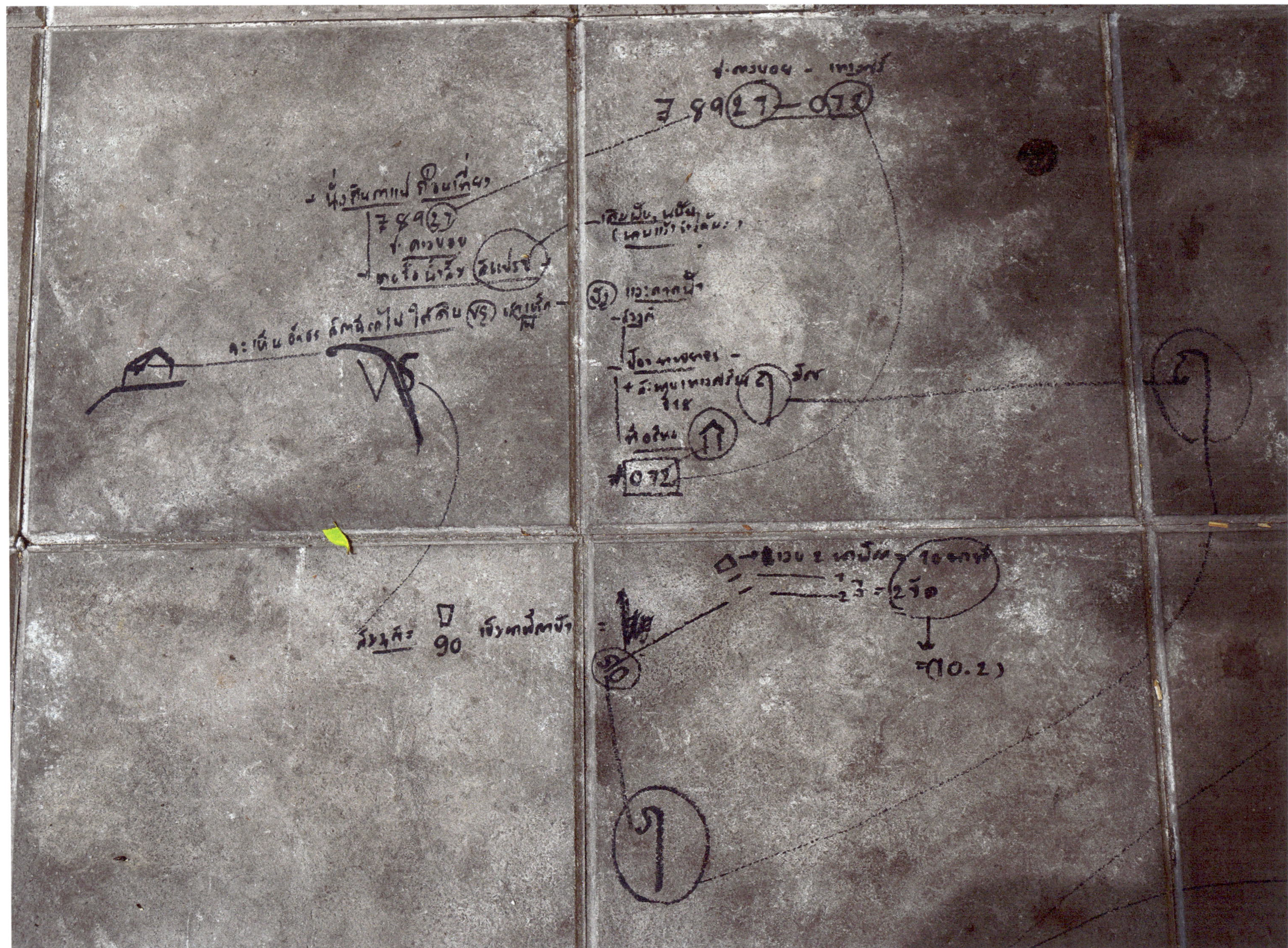

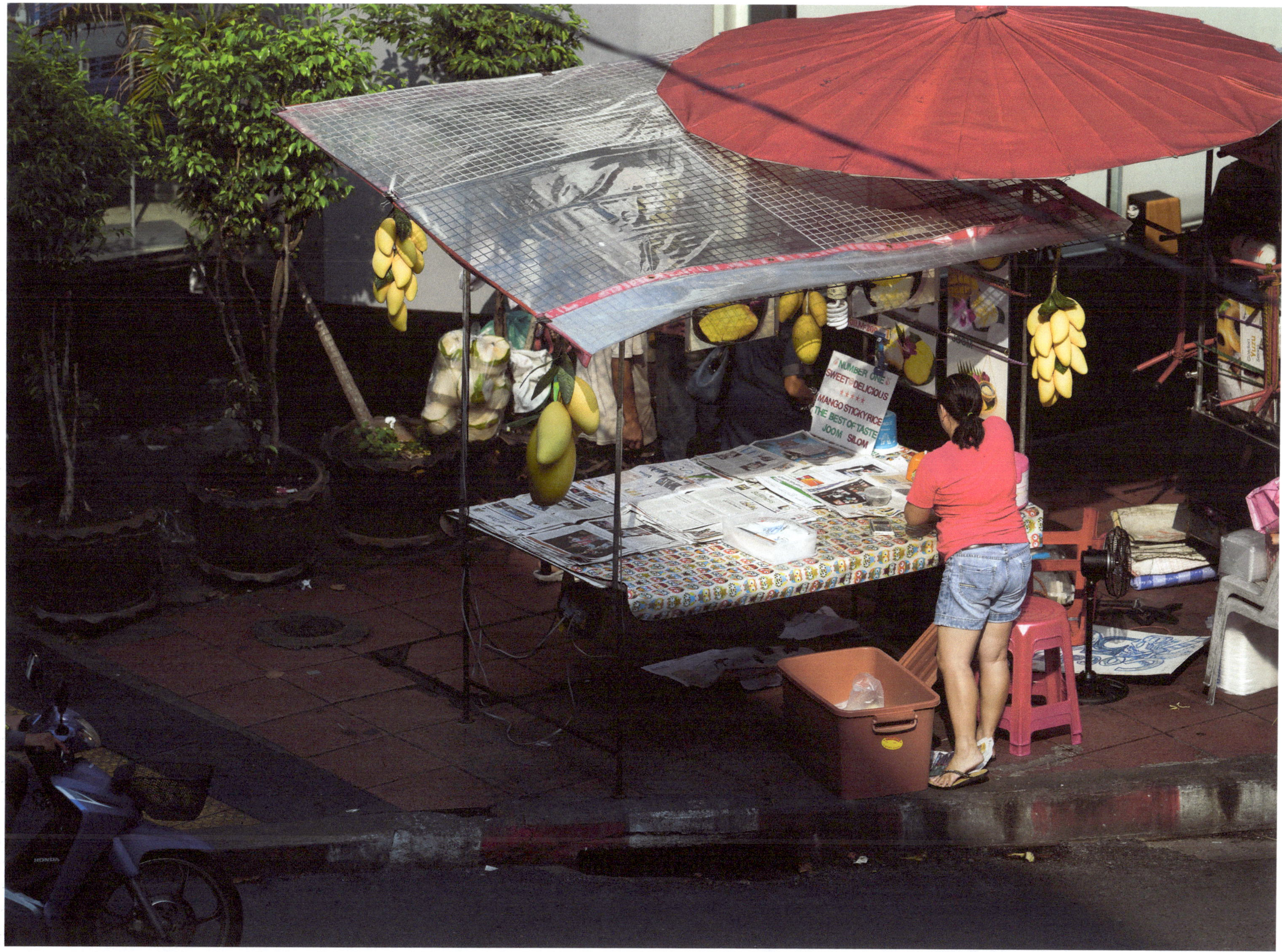
NUMBER ONE
SWEET DELICIOUS
★★★★★
MANGO STICKY RICE
THE BEST OF TASTE
JOOM SILOM

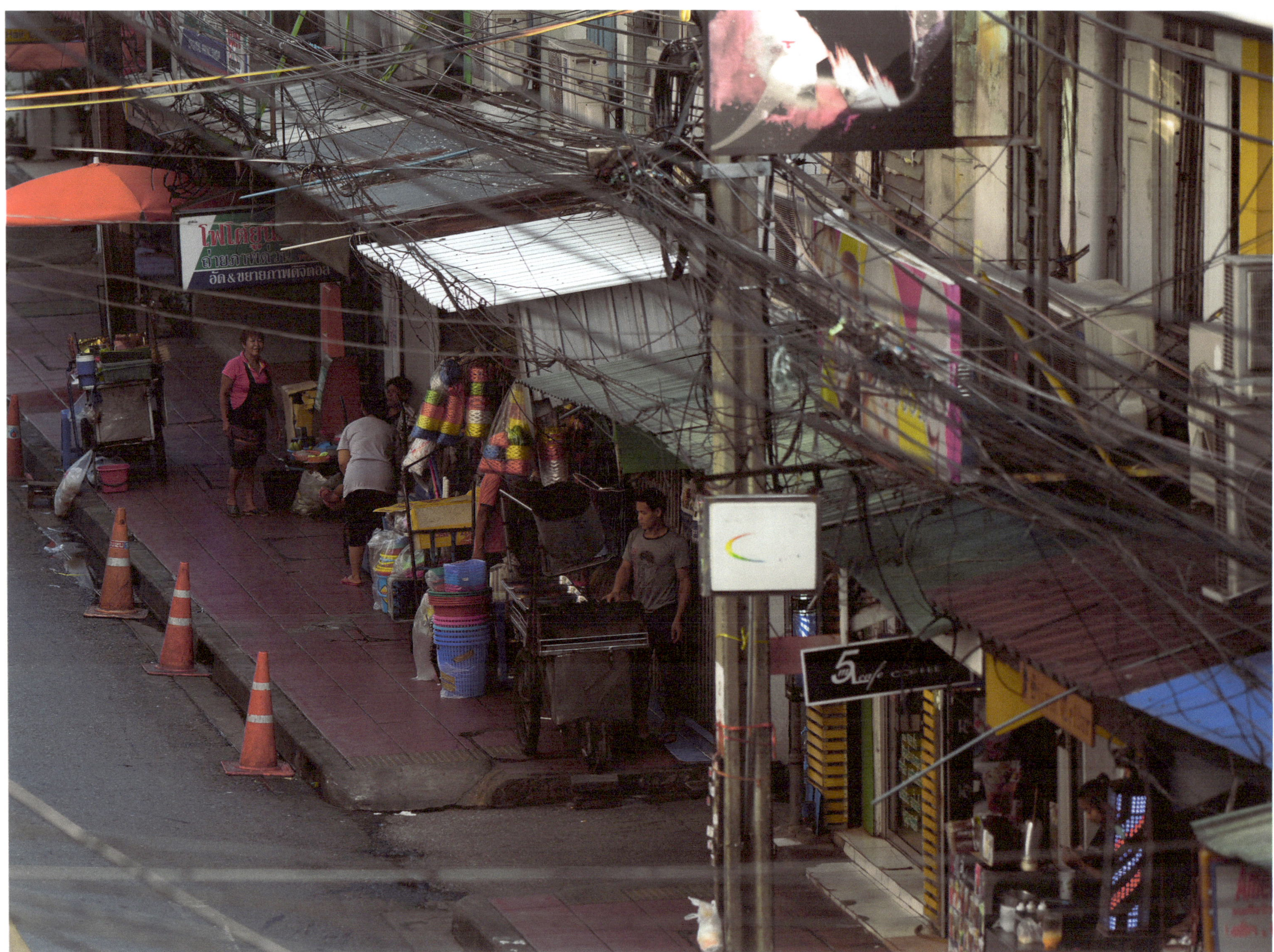

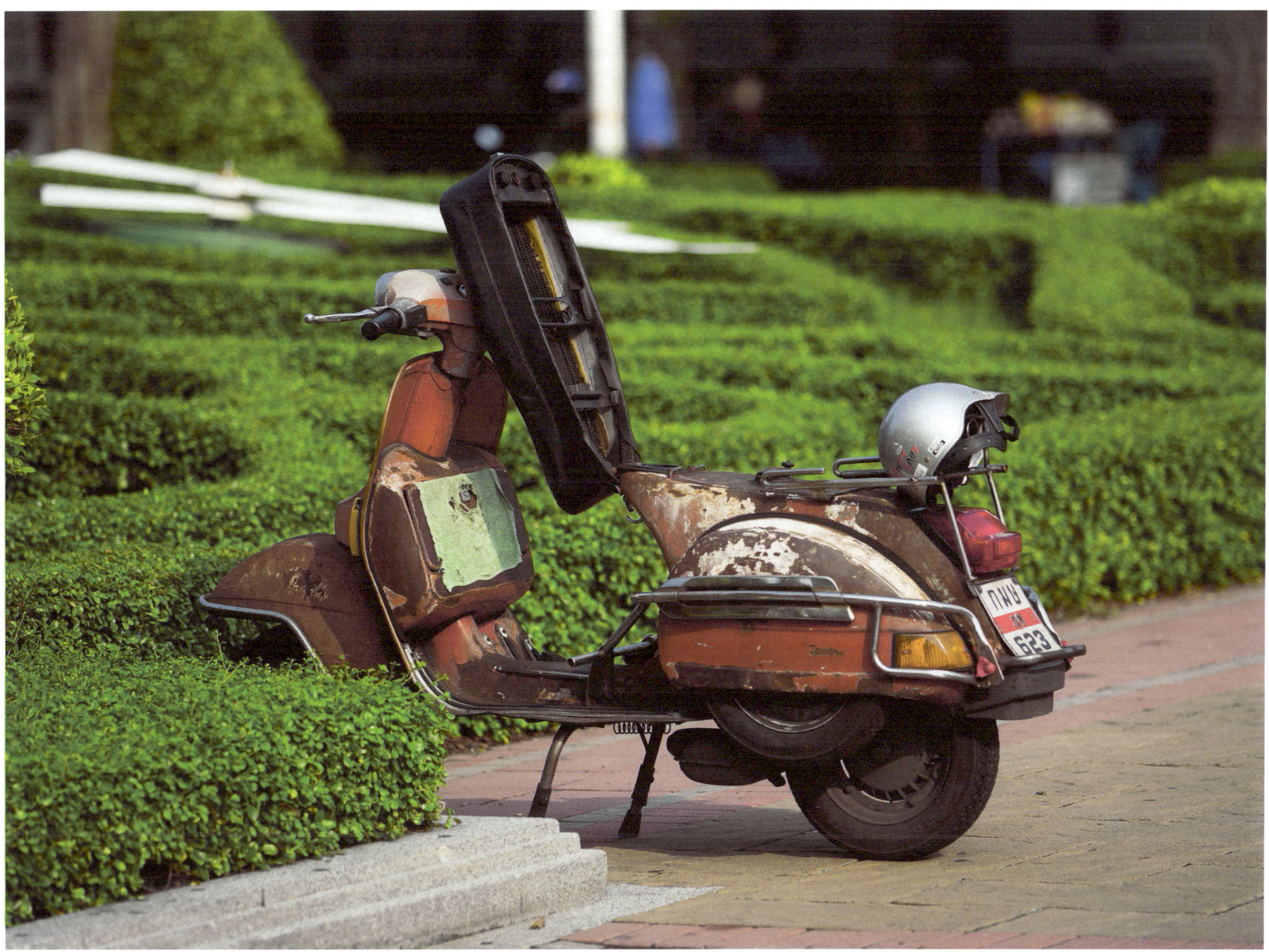
623

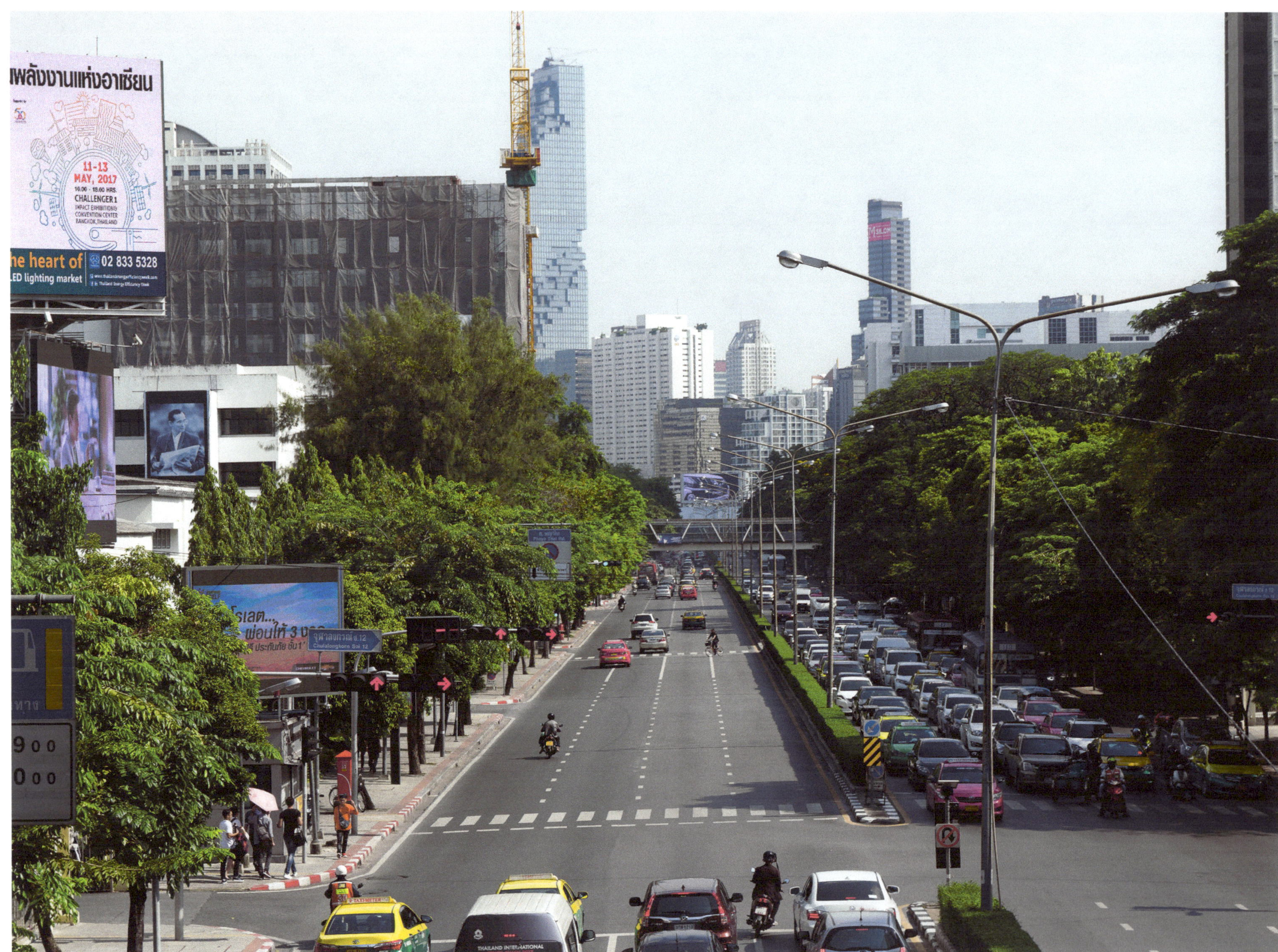
พลังงานแห่งอาเซียน
11-13
MAY, 2017
10.00 - 18.00 HRS.
CHALLENGER 1
IMPACT EXHIBITION&
CONVENTION CENTER
BANGKOK, THAILAND
he heart of
LED lighting market
02 833 5328
Chulalongkorn Soi 12

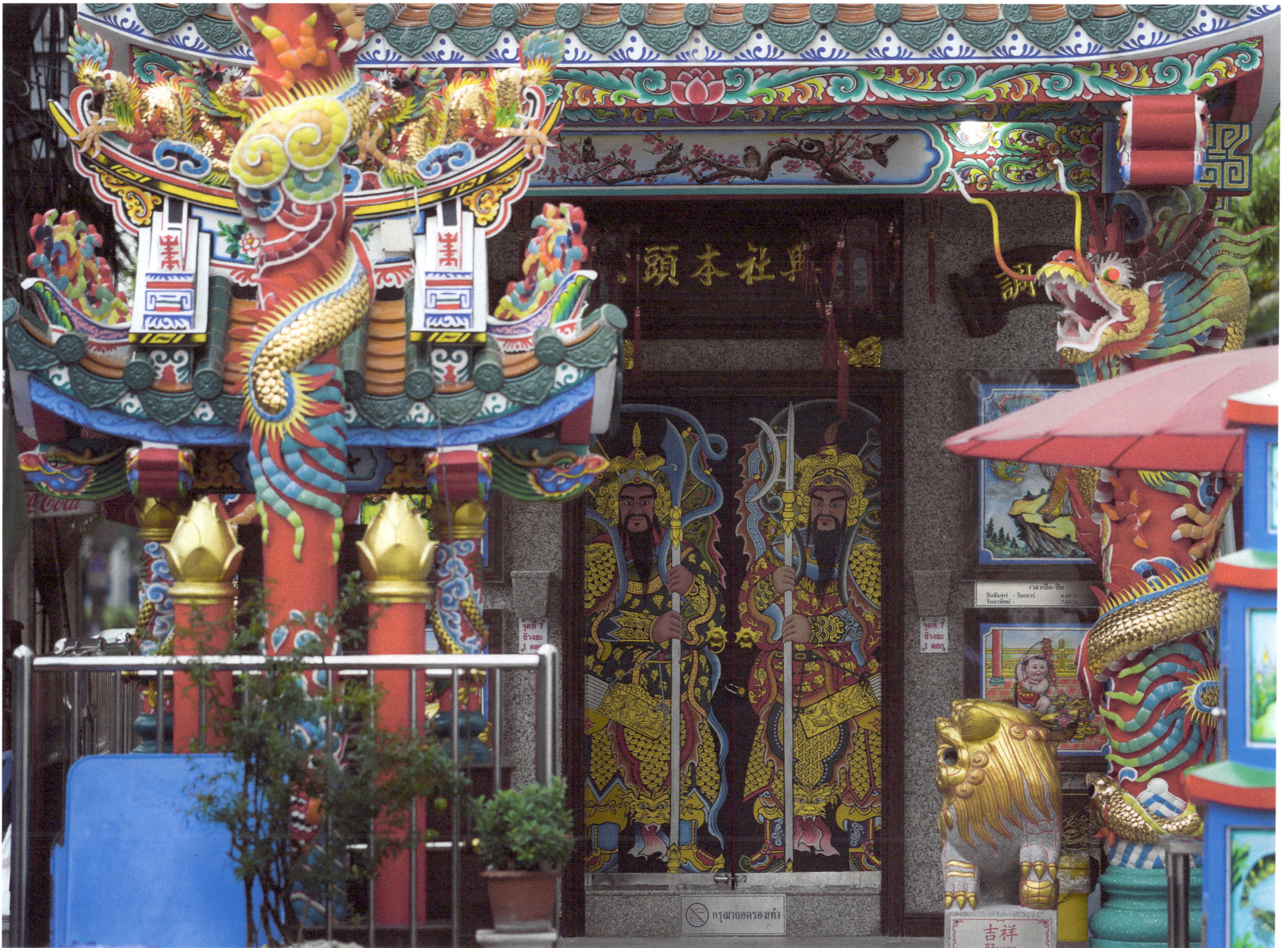
กรุณาถอดรองเท้า
吉祥

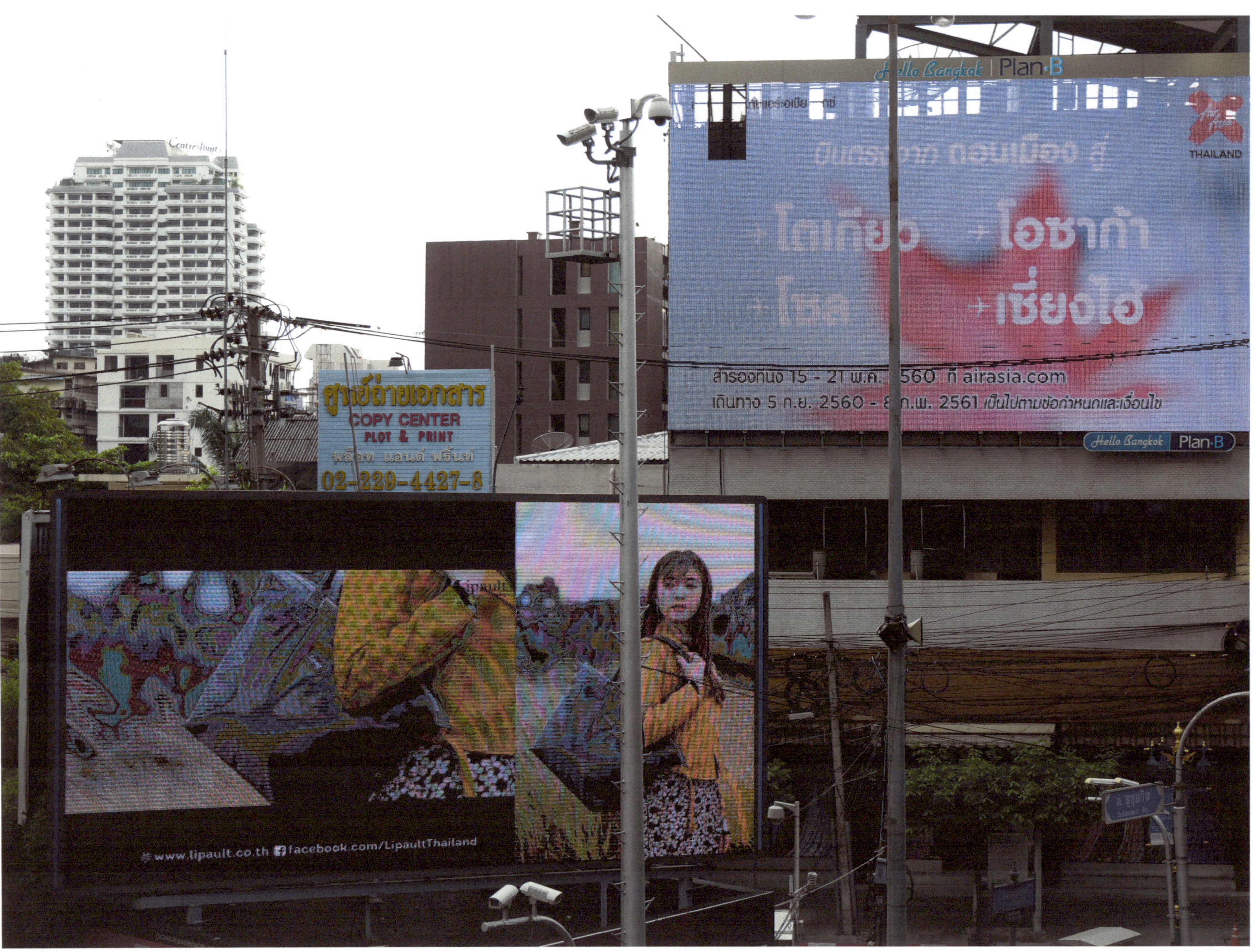
Hello Bangkok | Plan·B
THAILAND
ดอนเมือง สู่
โตเกียว
โอซาก้า
โซล
เซี่ยงไฮ้
airasia.com
เป็นไปตามข้อกำหนดและเงื่อนไข
Hello Bangkok | Plan·B
ศูนย์ถ่ายเอกสาร
COPY CENTER
PLOT & PRINT
พล็อท แอนด์ พริ้นท์
02-229-4427-8
www.lipault.co.th facebook.com/LipaultThailand

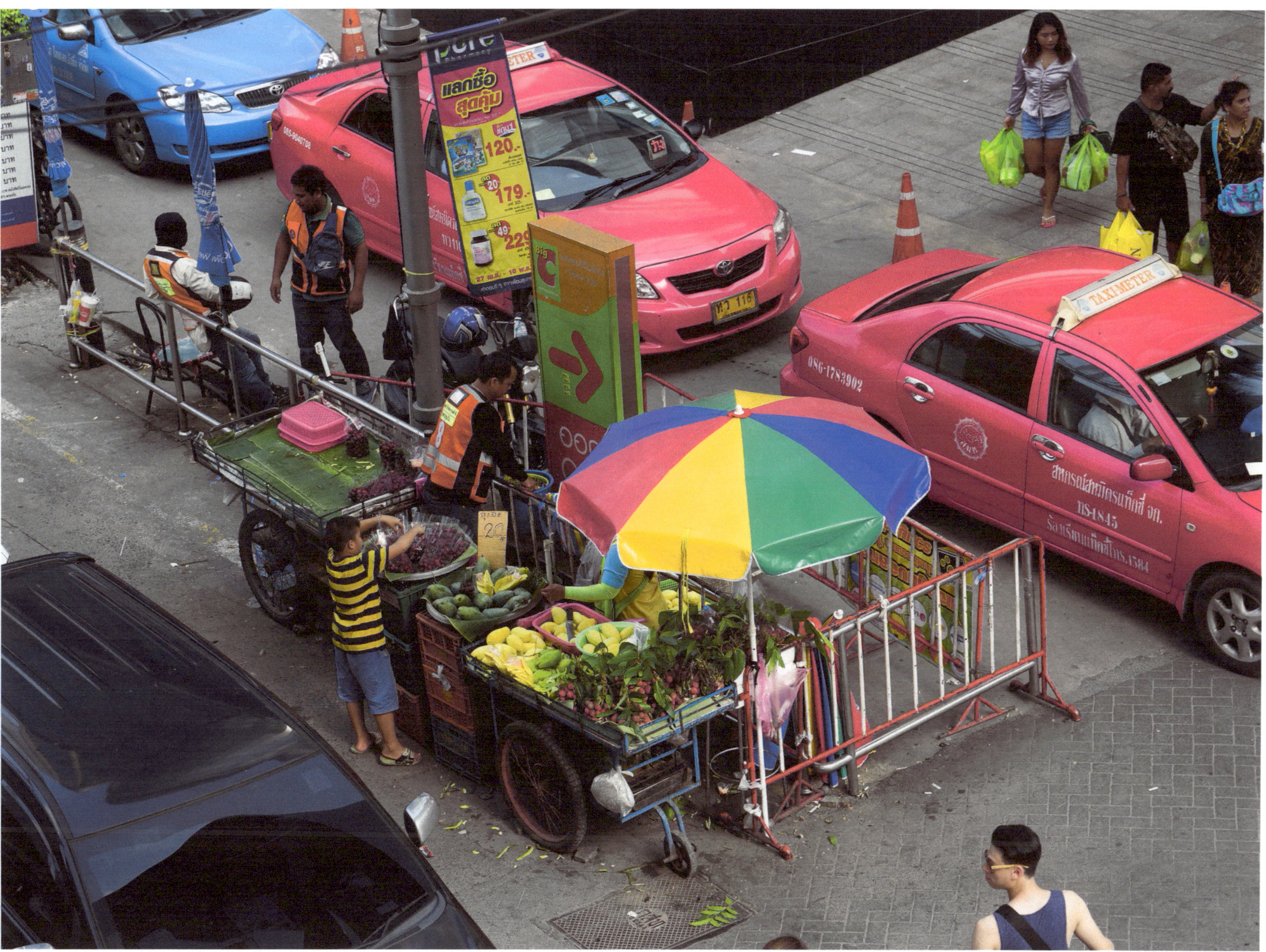
pure
pharmacy
แลกซื้อ
สุดคุ้ม
120.-
ลด 20
179.-
ลด 49
27 เม.ย. - 10 พ.ค.
TAXI-METER
086-1783902

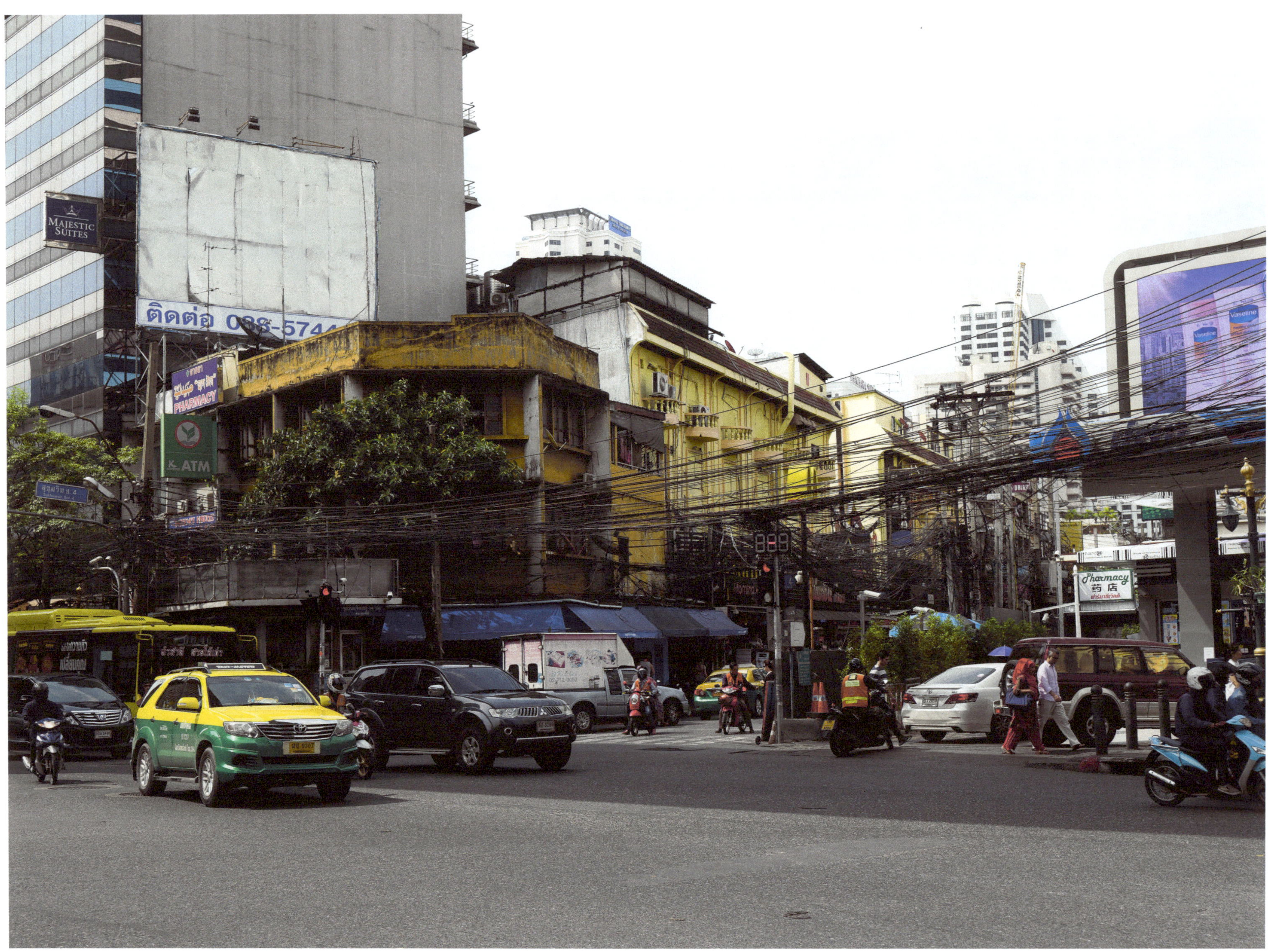
MAJESTIC SUITES
ติดต่อ 088-5744
PHARMACY
ATM
Pharmacy
药店

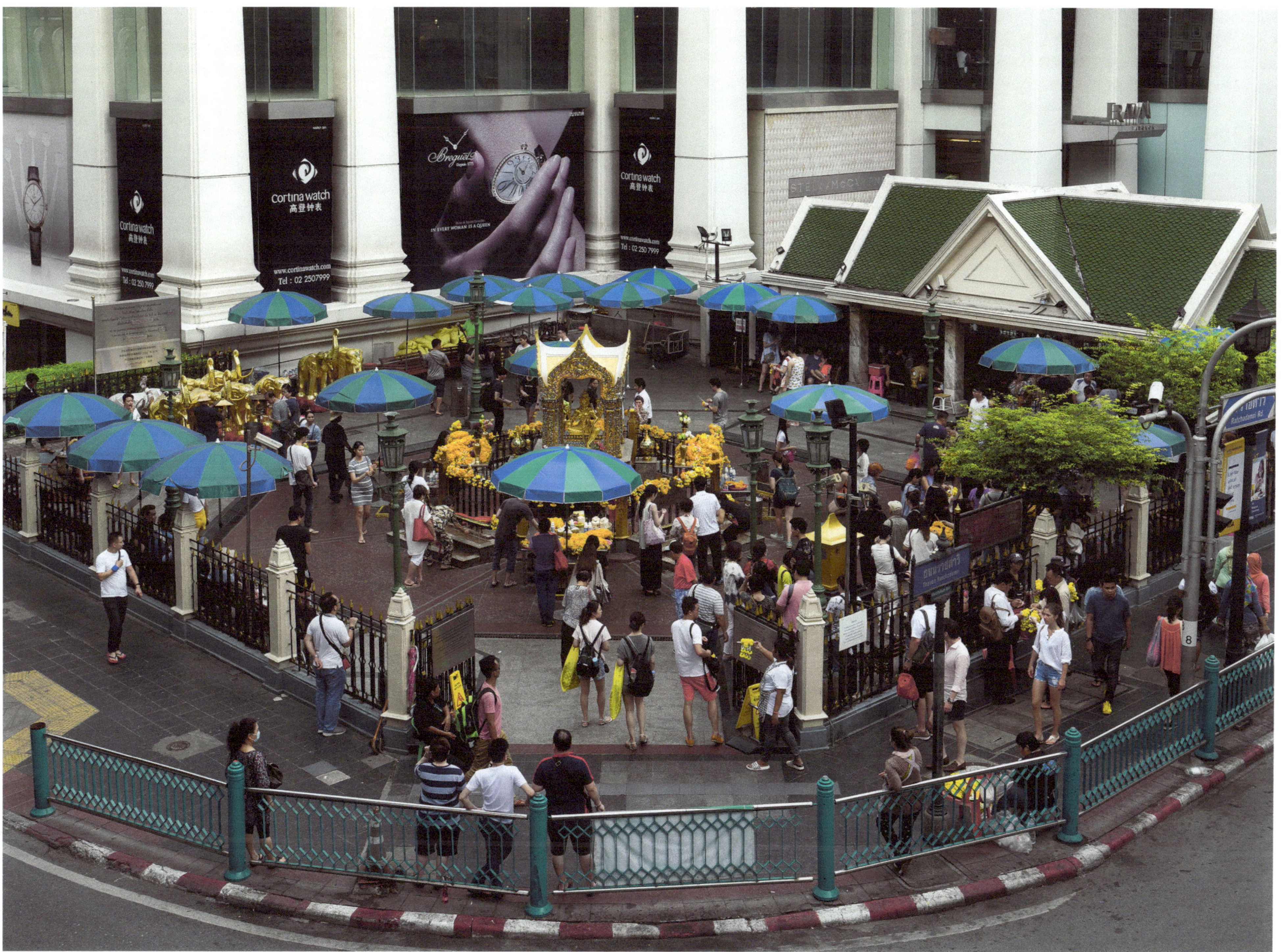
Cortina watch
高登钟表
www.cortinawatch.com
Tel : 02 2507999

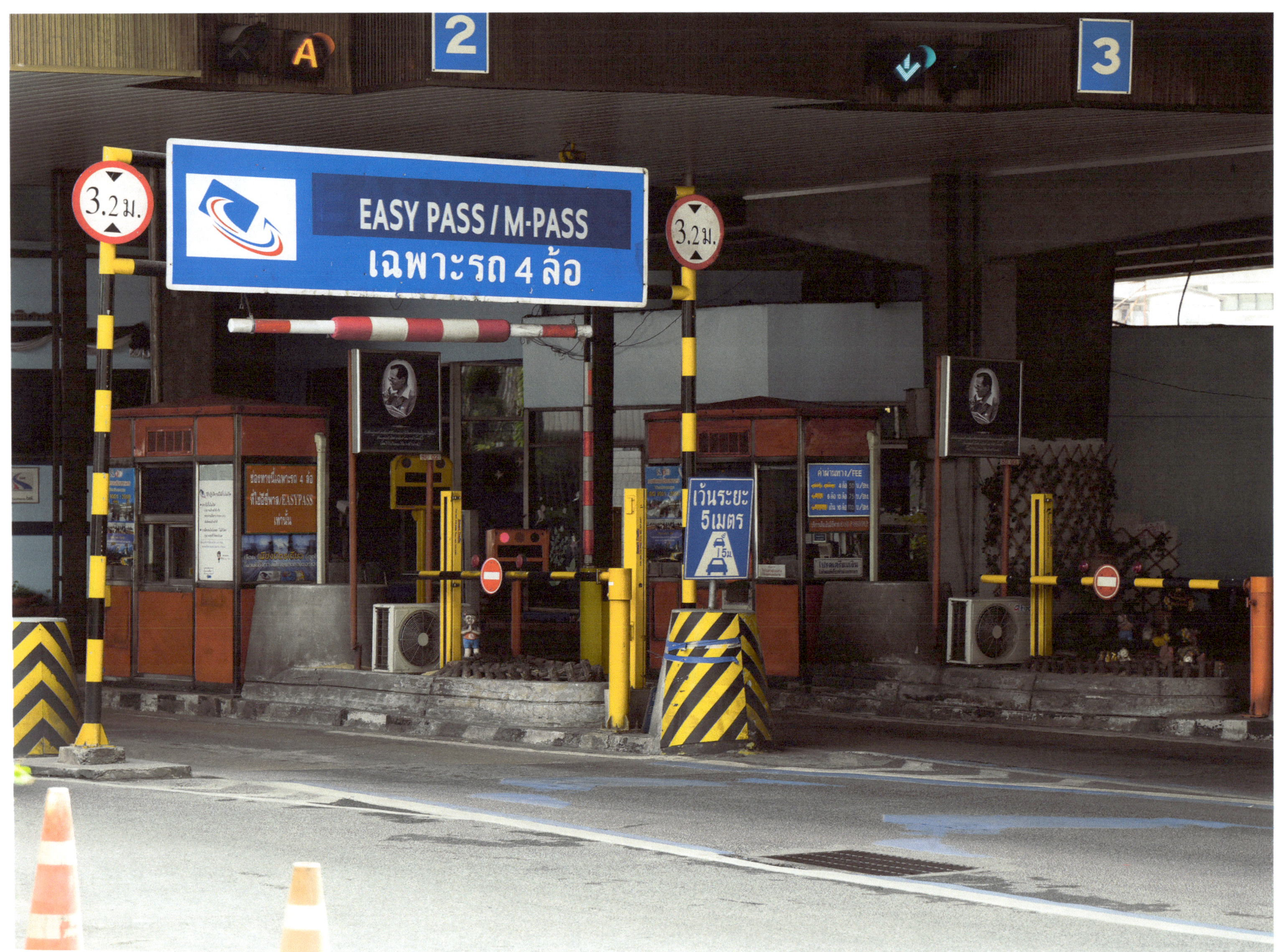

2
A
3
3.2ม.
EASY PASS / M-PASS
เฉพาะรถ 4 ล้อ
3.2ม.
เว้นระยะ
5เมตร
5ม.

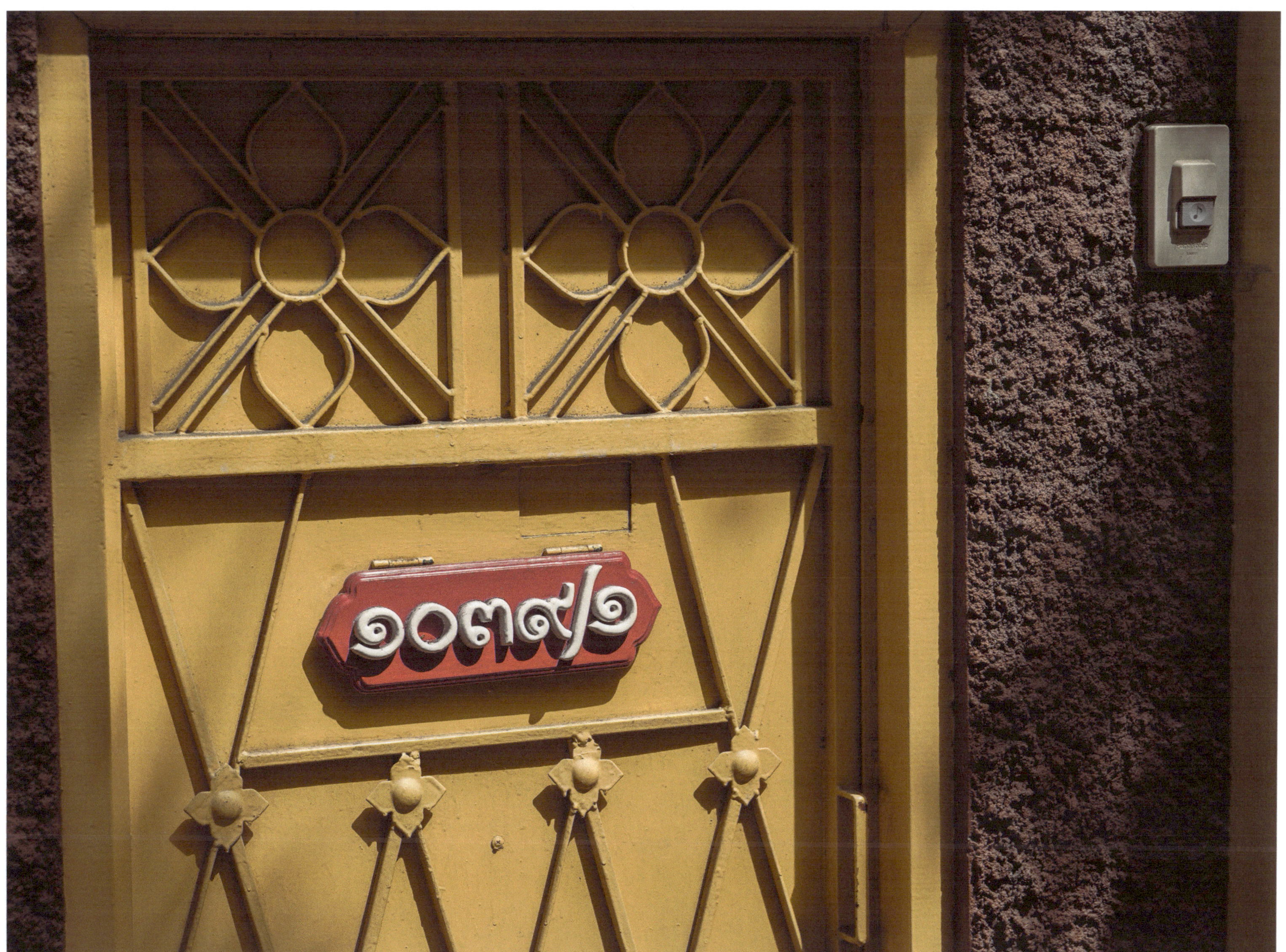
๑๐๓๙/๑

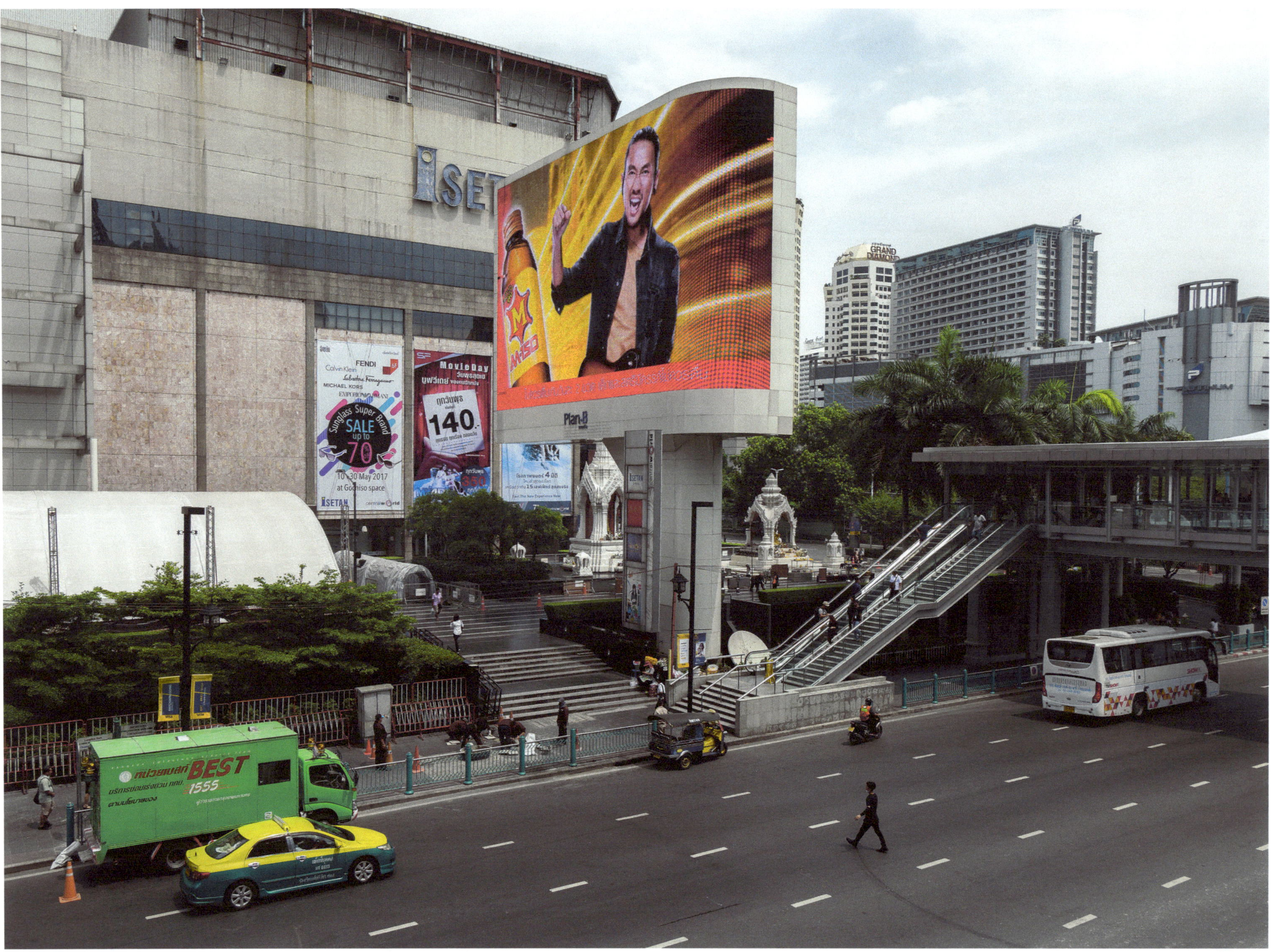
FENDI
Calvin Klein
Salvatore Ferragamo
MICHAEL KORS
6F
Sunglass Super Brand
SALE
up to
70
10 - 30 May 2017
at Gochiso space
ISETAN
centralwOrld
MovieDay
ทุกวันพุธ
140.-
Plan B
GRAND DIAMOND
BEST
1555

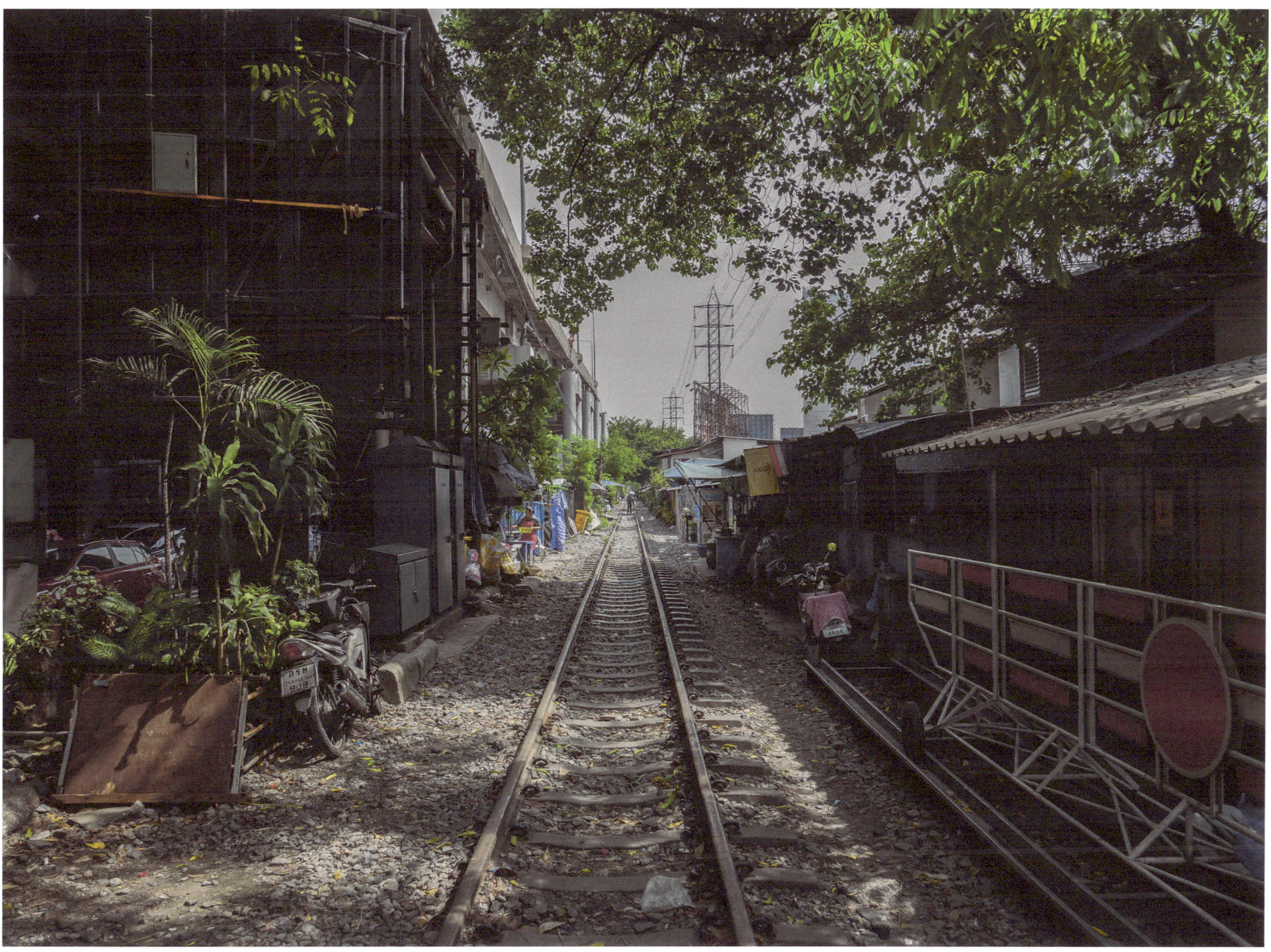

www.ingramcontent.com/pod-product-compliance
Lightning Source LLC
LaVergne TN
LVHW072331100826
845154LV00009B/150

* 9 7 8 0 9 9 8 0 6 8 2 2 0 *